Prison Life and the Aftermath of Thug Living

Prison Life and the Aftermath of Thug Living

Chaplain Training Approaches to Pastoral Care
for the Long-Term Incarcerated

DAMIEN W. D. DAVIS

Foreword by Sharon Ellis Davis

WIPF & STOCK · Eugene, Oregon

PRISON LIFE AND THE AFTERMATH OF THUG LIVING
Chaplain Training Approaches to Pastoral Care for the Long-Term Incarcerated

Wipf & Stock
An Imprint of Wipf and Stock Publishers
199 W. 8th Ave., Suite 3
Eugene, OR 97401

www.wipfandstock.com

PAPERBACK ISBN: 979-8-3852-2181-3
HARDCOVER ISBN: 979-8-3852-2182-0
EBOOK ISBN: 979-8-3852-2183-7

VERSION NUMBER 06/28/24

Contents

Foreword by Sharon Ellis Davis | vii
Acknowledgements | ix
Introduction | 1

Vision of the Carceral System | 4
    Context of Ministry | 4
    Theoretical Framework | 11
    Research & Literature Review | 14
    Objective, Implementation & Strategy | 23

Implementation | 29
    Effects of Violence on the Incarcerated | 30
    The Case Study | 34
    Examination | 35
    Evaluation | 42
    Data Gathering & Analysis Plan | 43
    Evaluation & Learning | 48

Consensus of 3 Cs Findings | 49
    Conclusion | 53

Survey for Formerly Incarcerated Individuals | 55
Survey for Chaplains | 58
Consent Form for Survey | 61
Bibliography | 65
Index | 67

Foreword

IT IS WITH GREAT pleasure and delight that I offer affirmation for the work of my former student, the Rev. Damien W.D. Davis, PhD, in this forward. This book stands as a testament to Damien's dedication to bridging the gap between theory and practice, scholarship and ministry, in the pursuit of advocating for the forgotten and marginalized within our society, who are also spoken about in religious spaces as the least, lost, and left out.

Damien and I first got to know each other after he was assigned to me, by his Professor, to serve as his advisor after completing his academic requirement. She believed he and I would connect well because of our experiences in chaplaincy. We both served as Chaplains, he a Chaplain within the Correctional System and I, formally as a Police Chaplain. Our connection was immediate, and I was enthusiastic to work with him on his vision for the ministry project he desired to engage in.

As a Chaplain deeply invested in the long-term care of prisoners, he brings a unique perspective to the forefront of discourse surrounding pastoral care within the prison system. His passion for ensuring the dignity and humanity of those serving life sentences resonates throughout these pages, as he delves into the complex dynamics of dehumanization and exclusion within the prison system. Drawing upon his extensive experience and scholarly engagement, Damien offers a compelling analysis of how individuals are systematically stripped of their humanity, transforming them into mere statistics rather than deserving recipients of compassion, empathy, and care.

Through research and insightful reflection, he sheds light on the subtle nature of biases and the urgent need for recognizing the inherent humanity of all individuals, regardless of their circumstances. With this knowledge he developed a model which introduces the care plan. He refers to it as the 3-C's. One of the most poignant aspects of Damien's work is his unwavering commitment to advocating for the rights and well-being of prisoners, even beyond the confines of the prison walls. While Damien may now serve as a hospice chaplain, his dedication to ensuring that prisoners are treated with love, empathy, and care, remains steadfast. This book serves as a powerful reminder that the values of genuine care and compassion know no bounds, transcending the limitations imposed by societal norms and institutional structures.

I wholeheartedly recommend this book to anyone involved in the field of prison ministry, from clinical pastoral educators to supervisors preparing chaplains for diverse settings, and encourage you to engage his work. Moreover, I believe that religious institutions and seminaries already engaged in prison ministry will find Damien's insights invaluable in shaping their approach to pastoral care within correctional facilities.

In conclusion, Damien's work is not merely a scholarly endeavor; it is a testament to the transformative power of empathy and compassion in the face of adversity. As our world grapples with the profound challenges of trauma and distress, this book serves as a beacon of hope, reminding us of the inherent value and dignity of every individual, especially those often overlooked and marginalized by society. With joy and enthusiasm, I commend this book to all who seek to cultivate a culture of care and compassion within our communities, recognizing that it is in extending love to the least among us that we truly embody the principles of justice and mercy.

Rev. Sharon Ellis Davis, M.Div., & Professor

Acknowledgements

For years, I've had the desire to research how chaplaincy can impact prison ministry. Through my late days, early moments, and a few missed events to make deadlines, my family has been extremely supportive of my efforts. To my wife Sharon Davis, when I wanted to give up or feeling unworthy about my project, I leaned on you to push me through. I love you. To my kids, Josiah, Macy, and Brooklyn Davis, thank you for giving daddy a hug and a kiss goodnight when I was typing. You just don't know how much that meant to me. To my parents, Pamela and Tyrone Davis, Sr., I could not have asked for better parents. To my brother Tyrone, Jr., thank you for always being a supporter of my endeavors. God blessed me with the gift of love and support in all you've done for me. To my father-in-law Joseph Okoh, God rest his soul, your son in law "Rev" did it! To my cousins EJ and Ryan, you were tragically taken from us. So, let this thesis be in honor of you and who you've been to me. To my advisor Rev. Dr. Sharon Ellis Davis, thank you for your advice and patience with me. I know I wasn't easy. To the distinguished professors of McCormick for your support, Rev. Dr. Stephanie Crumpton, Rev. Dr. Daniel Schipani, Rev. Dr. Delois Brown-Daniels, and Dr. Jenny McBride. To my conversational partners, Dr. Inna Mirsky and Rt. Rev. George Adamson, thank you for all your advice and wisdom. All of you have been instrumental in this project, so please accept my humble gratitude.

Introduction

CHAPLAINCY IN PRISON IS unlike any other experience one will have, and considering all its complexity, this population is unique. Typically, chaplaincy is viewed through the eyes of an individual caring for the sick in hospitals or providing services for veterans in retirement with every resource available. Serving as the mediator between the physician and family, chaplaincy typically tries to merge an idea of hopefulness for the unknown. The point of being a caregiver is to assist someone who has lost a loved one due to some tragic incident leading to death.

Now imagine being called to the bedside of an individual in custody convicted of murder, near his last breath of life, with no contact from a family member or friend to support them. This convicted person was the murderer of one of your family members due to having a disagreement or trying to gain props from their gang affiliation to be about that "thug life." To better understand what I mean, "thug life" is having a criminogenic behavior that physically and willfully commits harm that can be violent and lawless, which impacts the community. While that may be difficult to digest, you may know someone, or you can relate to the situation more closely. I, for one, did.

When preparing for this research project, on my last day of class, I received a call from a family member informing me my cousin was shot and killed during an altercation. Hurt, troubled, and disturbed, I felt my work of pastoral care toward individuals in custody was in vain. I could barely hold my head up because the tears of sadness would not stop. I began to question myself: "Why am I doing this?" And then, it was as if my family member came to me in a quiet voice saying, "people that hurt people are in pain." I could not figure it out, but then I recalled being summoned to the bedside of an individual in custody who asked me to pray for him.

He had been convicted of murder, and he could only utter from his lips, "Hey Chap, you think the Lord will forgive me for what I did?" I could not be permitted to dictate what God could do, even if it meant having to put my own bias I had at the moment to the side. This project not only became a personal journey but a desire to share my experience with other chaplains in corrections. Furthermore, I journeyed through the realm of corrections to discover a healthy and effective way of administering pastoral care to individuals in custody. In this task, I knew guidance became necessary, which meant even having to deconstruct how I provided pastoral care in prison.

In summary, this project brings together new knowledge that prepares prison chaplains in the environment to promote positive change and transformation. Thus, I created a methodology of pastoral care for chaplains working in prison called the 3 Cs (caution, care, and collaboration). This new methodology allows chaplains to harness an approach to gain the trust of the population they serve. The chaplain training model originated from a dialogue with formerly incarcerated citizens to listen to this community to understand what care they could have benefited from during their incarceration. This approach established the most pertinent themes for individuals in custody while listening to their stories and gaining the necessary empathy to respond pastorally to their challenges.

The misfortune is that society does not make room for grace and mercy to abide individuals in custody within the larger context. The "lock 'em up and throw away the key" punishment mentality must be dismantled. I believe the chaplains to be a necessary step in this challenge. The reality is that the individual in custody is someone's father, brother, cousin, or even friend. Therefore, one must closely monitor their judgment and perception of grace.

Furthermore, we must not allow our biases to prevent us from providing care to individuals in custody. Our mission is not to restrict one from gaining a closer relationship with themselves. Still, our mission is to offer the opportunity to reassure one of hope that addresses the trauma they face and become all that is good to the least of these. In this thesis, you will see the systematic ways I gathered information, developed the model for training based on data, and conducted successful training through the 3 Cs. This model for chaplains gave a specific structure to implement and incorporate a strategy to gain trust, develop empathetic listening skills, and find more effective ways to care for the long-term incarcerated.

Vision of the Carceral System

CONTEXT OF MINISTRY

FORMERLY A CHAPLAIN AT a maximum-security prison, part of my duties was being a religious coordinator for various religions. I started as a correctional officer seven years and have now been working as a chaplain for four years. The environment primarily consists of individuals in custody serving natural life who live in a six-by-eight-foot cell with bunkbeds with an attached toilet and sink. One desk (depending on the cell), one light attached to the ceiling near the cell's rear, and all enclosed behind steel bars facing the windows roughly twenty feet away. This is my day-to-day image of performing pastoral care throughout the institution.

Just about every stereotype one could think of regarding an individual in custody, I have allowed that perception to create bias before understanding that person's identity. The misfortune of that bias is that it can translate into a type of pseudo-reality that these individuals are subhuman. One thing I had to keep in mind as I viewed the individual in custody was not to see them as criminals but to look at them as created in the image of God. Despite what they have done, we have to consider the immediate need they face. An example would be being away from loved ones or perhaps even being unable to connect to society. Or being indigent (no one to place money in their books) and not receiving any support—all this can be a traumatic experience. These things have become a significant concern for people incarcerated because they have to rely solely on the state to provide for their basic needs. Before becoming a chaplain, I was a correctional officer for seven years, and I must say being in that position taught me a lot about myself. Firm, fair, and consistent was how officers intended to conduct themselves when dealing with individuals in custody.

More importantly, that perspective in some had prevented me from becoming the chaplain I desired to be because of the pseudo-reality of who I thought they were. They were often the complete opposite. I had to display the persona of a chaplain, someone called by God, and make that my active mission to fulfill. Therefore, I had the resilience to focus on the task and maintain my sense of purpose for being there because, to me, to do ministry is an opportunity to give incarcerated men a chance to thrive. Chaplaincy became my chance to shift from hopelessness to something that impacts them spiritually, socially, and mentally. While most men are seeking an opportunity at freedom, be it through clemency or seizing the moment to be pardoned, it is still, at times, piqued with the built-up anxiety of unknowingness.

By unknown, I mean the uncertainty of what type of prison environment one will walk into, good or bad. After individuals in custody are locked in a cell and sentenced to life in prison, will they feel they have nothing left to offer society or no reason to live? Often incarcerated persons will hear the disturbing news that their families can no longer afford to support them during their incarceration. Perhaps the unresolved trauma or overlooked mental health condition or drug abuse that has plagued them provides the reason to terminate their life. Or was their crime so heinous that even in their heart, they feared their life was in danger? Or, over time, perhaps one may feel anxiety about returning to society after being incarcerated for the last twenty to thirty years. Statistics have proven that in some cases, persons are likely to be released and others to remain incarcerated.

Even the idea of receiving little to no support causes the individual in custody to rely on the system to obtain their basic needs, e.g., cosmetics, can be disheartening. Especially when considering the anxiety of being placed in a cell with a stranger, constantly aware of the possibility that a physical assault may arise due to a disagreement or because the cellmate may suffer from a mental health condition he is unaware of. It is unfortunate that in this day in age, individuals in custody are loaded with the fear of losing their safety, well-being, and life during their incarceration. This harsh reality makes "doing time" mentally much more challenging to manage and, if dwelt upon, their future less optimistic. On a more positive note, I see men in prison who refuse to give up on themselves. They seek to find like-minded people to be with that try to encourage one another and learn how to build community within the prison system.

While in every environment there may be challenges in trying to befriend someone or build trust with someone to solve a communal problem to reach a common goal, the first goal for a chaplain is to create a rapport with the individual in custody. Many more concerns could be discussed, but the one thing in common they all have is trauma. Trauma affects those incarcerated differently than the rest of the world. Not having a visit, physical contact, or keeping up with the norm can damage the psyche, which drives one to despair. Individuals in custody, in a lot of ways, unintentionally cause one to withdraw from the normalcy of everyday life or even decline in their hygiene, as well as involve themselves in counterproductive behaviors.

If there are not any prosocial measures to assist in providing sustainability for their future, it makes their life much more challenging. It hinders their ability to develop better ways of approaching life differently. Just as their current residence has become their vehicle of damnation, their new outlook and perspective to revive their lives will become their salvation. Thus, navigating around the polemics as they arise becomes a strategic spiritual agenda of reimagining a world where they are humanized. When one is humanized, one begins to recognize one's self-worth and have a sense of purpose.

That purpose provides the determination to live, the decision to transform, and the determination to have the fortitude to re-identify oneself as made in the image of God. When one has time to self-reflect on what needs to change, the idea is to assist them in their capacity for that change. The goal of the chaplain when providing care to the individual in custody is to guide them in unpacking the resolution that resides in them. Furthermore, what should be dismissed from society's language is denying hope. For the incarcerated person, hope is more than just a word; it is the anchor that provides the reason to accept an alternative.

That alternative is being spiritually equipped to grapple with the prison environment and hoping to find a voice that addresses their turmoil. Therefore, every engagement the chaplain has with an individual in custody must have a spiritual component with a positive impact. As a chaplain, my role became vital to the individuals in custody because they were questioning, "Will God be with me during this journey of my life? Has God forgotten about me? Has society forgotten about me?" Thus, my context is made up of one thousand men who are serving twenty-plus years to natural life in prison and also short-term sentences within a maximum-security prison. They reside in a six-by-eight-foot cell behind steel bars, two men to a cell while sleeping on steel bunk beds.

My primary functions require me to respond to requests made by individuals in custody regarding religious diets, religious jewelry, marriage, inquiring about religious services, and seeking pastoral care. These themes are essential to their needs because they are tangible things that connect them to the outside world. But, from an internal perspective, these things do not fill the void of loneliness and despair. For years they have been accustomed to one method of coping: reactive. Reactive in this environment is maintaining old concepts. Instead of resolving conflict through conversing or finding other means, violence remains their mode of expression.

To some degree being reactive instead of initiative-taking has ultimately sabotaged their freedom. Individuals in custody believe this was the only language their community understood because being initiative-taking in the prison context doesn't appear to produce immediate results. Instead, being aggressive or taking preventative measures does not have the same effect as explaining to someone physically the seriousness of the situation. One argument some have alluded to is that individuals in custody struggle with some form of PTSD. One could argue that their conviction and the trauma they have inflicted on themselves or inflicted on others have created an intensely stressful predicament, causing an unfathomable disorder that they have not discovered how to address.

Take, for example, situations where one is threatened or their character is attacked due to miscommunication: two individuals compromised by a fictitious rumor of being involved in a same-gender loving activity. To the outside world, the LGBTQ community has wildly become accepting of persons of that particular sexual orientation. However, the stigma that incarcerated men will inevitably become sexually attracted to other men in prison is false. Although prison rape does occur, it does not fall within the same category of willing individuals in custody who are attracted to the same sex.

Therefore, in a male institution, men must maintain their masculinity, but this view must be broad instead of narrow. They must always have the appearance of strength that is absent of fear. It is already troubling for them to be stereotyped by society, so to add further discriminating themes is an attack on their character that is offensive in their world. As a result of it being offensive mentally in their world, one could only imagine the damage it does to them spiritually. The desire to be heard but not be heard impacts them in ways that serve more as a method of injustice toward their development as human beings.

So, contextually this means learning how to give those without a voice the space to exercise their perspective. Learning how to create spaces where their premonitions are validated despite their conditions is essential. The comparison of our lifestyle to theirs is drastically different because the primary thing that citizens overlook is their freedom. Staff that enter prisons every day do not face having the option to leave or attend their loved one's funeral. Staff also have the option of what they are going to wear.

Imagine being told what to eat or being told when to sleep. Imagine being told when you can exit your quarters or breathe fresh air. It is unimaginable because society has failed to realize our luxury as occupants in the United States, and the idea of being stripped of these luxuries is baffling. Some of the most minute things we take for granted are magnetized within the prison. This teaches me how to be humble and sensitive to their humanity. I have examined various other concepts to assist me in exploring how pastoral care is a relevant tool to bring a sense of normalcy to the institution and how chaplains across the state can better prepare themselves.

But it is equally necessary to pragmatize these scenarios to understand where individuals come from. They come from an environment that feeds on toxicity. While some thrive on creating chaos, the majority have become reclusive to acts that misrepresent who they are and desire to be. In more cases than less, they no longer have the infatuation of being deemed a menace to society. One particular person, whom I will refer to as "Ahmad," had succumbed to suicidal ideation and made a suicide attempt; I had placed him in a pro-social environment of spiritual as well as mental programming classes.

Unfortunately, this individual had been so accustomed to poor decision-making that he believed his only alternative was to take an excessive number of drugs. One statement I recall from our conversation is, "I'm not used to normal. How do you'll do it? It's hard trying to get my life together because I'm so used to f****** it up?" As alarming as that statement was, I had to take heed of his honesty and transparency. He had been so use to abuse and trauma that his desire to reconnect with positive behaviors of being free that finding a new way of looking at life was foreign. I had to find ways of reconnecting him to his value in the world and how to find value in himself for his well-being.

Thus, the desire to reconnect with the outside world and to positively address the polemics that have contributed to their stagnation becomes the focus. They feel pain as much as anyone else, so they want to disconnect themselves from old ways of thinking.

They want to be something more normal where they can have the same respect and admiration as one living beyond the walls of confinement. While psychological measures can redirect an individual in custody to where they want to be, spiritually, one also wants to learn how to hold themselves accountable. Spiritually, I also needed to get him to channel his identity with God and allow him to foster what that looks like in the community.

Pastoral care in prison can then become the guide where one will spiritually reflect on their current lifestyle and journey with others who are on the same trajectory as they are. These men have the potential to rediscover who they are by actively reimagining what they want the world to know about them. The memory of the traumatic experience they faced before their incarceration has caused them to feel hopeless for the future. Therefore, the chaplain's responsibility in this context gives them a glimpse of a reality they can reach together. While the journey is primarily up to them, for them to know they're not alone as they work through their difficult circumstances gives them the courage to want more and creates an expectation for themselves.

Therefore, the chaplain's responsibility in this context gives them a glimpse of a reality they can reach together. While the journey is primarily up to them, knowing they're not alone as they work through circumstances gives them the courage to want more and creates an expectation for themselves. In this ministry project, you will see how I conducted this research and the implementation of how I utilized my 3 Cs concept: caution, care, and collaboration. You will hear the conversation of those formerly incarcerated, chaplains currently working in the prison system, and what conclusion was drawn. Within this discovery, you will see how this newfound methodology provides a clinically driven and religious response for chaplains working in prison to offer better care. And you will learn how this impact can serve as a model for future training for others who desire to inspire and motivate individuals in custody. I hope this project becomes a framework for us to consider another way of incorporating an actual merger between chaplaincy and psychology.

THEORETICAL FRAMEWORK

Chaplains are considered caretakers because our perspective utilizes tools to administer the care needed and ensure empathy is being transmitted toward spiritual growth. Pastoral care within the prison is more complex yet humbling. Regardless of what men were convicted for, every encounter should be viewed through the lens of recognizing their humanity and one created in the image of God. By this concept, pastoral care in prison is to become less critical of their past and committed to engaging in their spiritual development for the future. As a result, I had to assess my leadership style and approach protecting others better with humility.

This style is reflected in how I would help others by offering my resources to create normalcy, advocating for the men incarcerated and always finding opportunities that facilitated their ability to manage self-care. My style had evolved due to how I've previously conceptualized theology in prison and learned to understand its theological framework. Theology within my context was complicated and trans-cultural at the same time, which meant being cautious, careful, and collaborative when approaching situations. Moreover, the trans-cultural concept conceptualizes what they need best within the prison culture and how to maintain boundaries when offering pastoral care.

Through this, I encouraged every encounter to become an opportunity of building and displaying a sense of integrity. Furthermore, a chaplain must perceive a person's current state as having the capacity to transform their cultural ideology intentionally: though I am incarcerated, I choose not to conform to the prison mentality. My methodology of pastoral care resembles the scriptural reference Col 1:21–23 which says, "And you who were once estranged and hostile in mind, doing evil deeds, he has now reconciled in his fleshly body through death, to present you holy and blameless and irreproachable before him—provided that you continue securely established and steadfast in the faith, without shifting from the hope promised by the gospel that you heard, which has been proclaimed to every creature under heaven. I, Paul, became a servant of this gospel."

The incarcerated men have been cast out of their community, their future dictated by a judge's sentence, and the family they once knew begins to drift away slowly. Thus, my theological challenge is how prison chaplains should foster a better hope for them. Agents of change are called to advocate against despair, promote care, and be able to recognize individuals in custody are people seeking to establish peace within themselves, their community, and with God. Traditional intersectionality is characterized as the theory of overlapping social identities such as race, gender, sexuality, and class that contribute to specific types of systemic oppression and discrimination experienced by an individual. One of the main themes is that individuals in custody feel they face oppression and discrimination, as they both prompt a display demeaning one's humanness.

In retrospect, intersectionality in corrections toward individuals in custody has variations froms of oppressive and discriminatory practices, where society systematically forecasts its judgment. The gap between those incarcerated and those living in the "free world" is isolated to the specific locations that make them socially disconnected from understanding what it means to be human. According to Kimberlé Crenshaw, "Intersectionality is just a metaphor for understanding the ways that multiple forms of inequality or disadvantage sometimes compound themselves, and they create obstacles that often are not understood within conventional ways of thinking about anti-racism or feminism or whatever social justice advocacy structures we have."[1] An example of that in my context of prison ministry is the complications of addressing the problems and concerns between staff toward the individuals in custody. One apparent theme is the notion of how one is being identified and trying to shift away from the perceived image.

Perception within corrections is "pseudo" because it gives an idea that the illusion one has stemmed from perceived inception. However, when one focuses on the evident concerns and care of the individual, it allows an opportunity to manifest into awareness.

1. Crenshaw, "What is Intersectionality?"

This awareness, as much as it is a problem, is the idea of "being seen" and the idea of "being present." A chaplain being seen indicates individuals in custody are observing the actions and absence based on the lack of encounters. A chaplain being present is to be jointly engaged in the affairs, meet the individual in custody in their despair, and journey with them for a positive outcome.

With that positive pro-social change in place, in the end, it dismantles the institutional mentality of incarceration as a norm and steers one away from recidivism. One thing that must be understood is the impact of those serving long-term or short-term sentences are seeking ways to prevent recidivism. However, the primary issue is that they focus on short-term satisfaction and have less regard for a long-term consequence in response to their actions. Consider the lens of faith and spirituality regarding the statement made by the criminal on the cross. The awareness was that this man felt he deserved punishment. His only request was that "Jesus remember me when you come into your kingdom."[2]

Just because men are incarcerated doesn't mean they don't seek the spiritual component to revive them. Thus, the position of the gospel was designed to promote growth and to rebuild a better relationship with: God, humanity, and self. This brought me to the understanding that the intersectionality of corrections should address qualitative research that uses a multi-method. To better articulate this theory, it means that "qualitative researchers study things in their natural settings, attempting to make sense of, or interpret, phenomena in terms of the meaning people bring to them."[3] In theory, a multi-method understanding has more flexibility and focuses on the general nature of deciding what best fits in providing care.

Most conversations around incarceration are either ways of reducing recidivism or mass incarceration. While these are significant issues, men who have committed crimes seeking rehabilitation or the desire to re-enter back into society are forgotten. Community in itself gives harsh criticism that is embellished with a deep-rooted

2. Luke 23:41–42.
3. Sensing, "Qualitative Research," 57.

bias, making means of rehabilitation much more difficult to accept. This causes mixed emotions in society regarding who should be taken and who should be redeemed. Ideally, metanarrative aids in describing what scholar values, determines, and provides the motivation to believe it's just as important as it is worthy.[4]

Although my theological belief is rooted in Christian values, I utilized a humanistic approach to examine one's moral compass. Thus, the focal point was to enhance one's skill set and reinforce an idea that absolves them from engaging in counterproductive activities. From a religious approach, I drew from the Gospel of Luke 23:42: "Jesus, remember me when you come into your kingdom." What makes this act of solicitation important is that the thief was asking Jesus to take a mental note in that moment of recollection of the space that they were in. The criminal on the cross entrusted Jesus, whom presumably he may have never met, had the audacity of hope to request that he'd be remembered beyond the space they once were present in.

RESEARCH & LITERATURE REVIEW

To further elaborate on the necessity of having chaplain training explicitly tailored for prison ministry becomes a critical message of dispelling the misfortune individuals in custody have and recognizing our mistakes of not advocating for them. The following scholars that I felt portrayed to have a consistent theme that crosses over into my context were: Tim Sensing, William Badke, Mary Clark Moschella, Emily R. Brault, Shadd Maruna, Louise Wilson, Kathryn Curran, Don S. Browning, Terry D. Cooper, Maria Duffy, Linda Lee Smith Barkman, Sadie Pounder, Ray Anderson, and Virginia Holeman. Their examples assisted me with my dialogue as they addressed important matters concerning my research project. In addition to this project, I utilized the following to address other theological disciplines, such as Michelle Clifton-Soderstrom,

---

4. Badke, *Research Strategies*, 27.

Dominique Gillard, Harold Trulear, and Jenny McBride. All of which have two things in common.

They've instructed individuals in custody on aspects of various seminary frameworks (i.e., bible, church history, ethics, theology, liturgics, pastoral care, homiletics, and Christian education). They have personally impacted those in custody by how the systemic role of incarceration needs to be a therapeutic agenda to better those in prison. The crucial question they all addressed was the question, "How does one identify with the incarcerated community?" These dialog partners provided clarity and the concern that individuals in custody face, as well as what they continue to grapple with while in prison. Another area of focus was the narrative theory presented by Tim Sensing because it would help me facilitate and interpret how to address individuals in custody concerns by helping build their spiritual in conjunction with psychological care.

With this interpretive phenomenon, narrative theory brings us to the discussion surrounding pastoral care in prison. Ideally, the goal of narrative therapy is to give them permission to be transparent and transcend the presumption of being permanently hopeless. To better ascertain this idea, Virginia Todd Holeman believed that the most effective therapy relies on the client and practitioners "to remain grounded in God, seek to be open to the inspiration of the Holy Spirit, and conduct their work in a manner that is God-honoring."[5] This would suggest that one's experience brings awareness that proceeds from their illuminated awakening, perhaps causing a great shock by shifting from their present reality into something to look forward to. Not only that, but their experience also reinforces them to process their concerns cognitively and encourages them to interpret that moment and for every encounter to be restorative.

Not only that, but our target as professionals in the field of chaplaincy is to be both the Christian influencer and apply reasonable psychological practices that speak to the individual as a whole. Therefore, our obligation cannot be seeking validation for

5. Holeman, "Theology for Better Counseling," 77.

our methods but raising questions that respond to one's faith tradition and give clarity to contemporary perspectives.

To assist me in addressing the social and cultural framework of prison ministry, I began with what Shadd Maruna refers to as "an adaptive mechanism that helped to resolve psychological conflict" and thus moved to "resolve emotional ambivalence."[6] This aspect addressed the long-term condition of building a new foundation based upon an unexpected future. With the motivation of seeking a new identity, Tom O'Conner affirms that the "absence of research on the rehabilitative effect of religion on adult offenders is surprising given that religious involvement has been found to be positively associated with social conformity and with adjustment within prison."[7]

One trajectory of these social constructs is found in Angola. This Louisiana prison was known for being one of the most violent prisons in America, where 90% of the men incarcerated will never return to society. However, scholars Michael Hallett, Bryon Johnson, Joshua Hays, Sung Joon Jang, and Grant Duwe discovered that the goal was to seek moral rehabilitation by equipping men with a sacred responsibility. Socially, the men are "governed by a personalist ethic of what they call 'Relationship Theology.' Angola's Inmate Ministers strive to serve both staff and their fellow inmates through focused attention to interpersonal relationships."[8] Looking deeper to provide other means more connected contextually to what prison theology looks like, I refer to scholars who were active participants in addressing the theological frameworks and constructed similar careful examinations of the overarching concepts individuals in custody faced.

For starters, Linda Barkman of Fuller Theological Seminary believes that "prison theology is about how prisoners think of their condition, community, and whole life span in light of their

6. Maruna, Wilson, and Curran, "Why God Is Often Found Behind Bars," 174.

7. O'Conner, "Impact of a Volunteer Prison Ministry Program."

8. Hallett, et al., "U.S. Prison Seminaries," 153.

experience of God and the gospel."[9] This is important because there is a theory that those incarcerated have very few opportunities. But on the contrary, God already exists in that context. The focus of the gospel is speaking to their pain of crime, sin, and victimization, and the impact of their incarceration has become a challenge to their spiritual growth. She also argues that "unlike many congregations in the community who need to be convinced that they are sinners, the issue with prisoners is not in convincing us that we are sinners, it is in convincing us that we are salvageable, redeemable."[10]

Thus, the focus would be to intentionally bring forth care that carefully argues they are still worthy of redemption and life in God's sight. Dominique Gillard suggests, "Where the law demanded punishment, Jesus offers grace. Where the law required bloodshed, Jesus calls for restoration, repentance, and forgiveness. Where the law suggests that order comes through purging out the criminal, Jesus shows us that order is restored when our communities are reconciled."[11] In retrospect, men incarcerated for crimes they didn't commit would mirror the narrative of a biblical character, such as Joseph being wrongfully accused of a crime he didn't commit and having to deal with the depression of not knowing what their outcome will be.

The misfortune of individuals in custody wrongfully convicted is deemed with a penurious ideology that, due to past behaviors, is a form of recourse for retribution. With the complexity of this idea, one has, "Is this the Lord's will to receive a payback for the wrong I've done?" As unethical and immoral as it is, society has this mentality and has adopted this systemic prejudice as a means to validate itself of not continuing on the path of criminal behavior. Instead of mirroring themes to formulate opinions not properly placed based on fact, the crucial role of chaplains is to address the immediate situations as they are and not what we anticipate

---

9. Barkman, "Towards a Missional Theology of Prison Ministry," 40.

10. Barkman, "Towards a Missional Theology of Prison Ministry," 41.

11. Gilliard, "Rethinking Incarceration," 58–59.

them to be. For this reason, we can't prescribe our thoughts what we presume of their past.

Our role is to adhere to the present circumstances of being forced to live and confined to a system that has already dictated one's outcome in life. Another scholar who explored the dimensions of what prison theology should look like—and its goals—is Sadie Pounder. To better articulate these dimensions, she suggests that "prison theology is contextual theology; it seeks to determine the actual nature of the context and respond to that context from the perspective of the Christian faith."[12] This doesn't mean approaching various perspectives of religious frameworks with one type of ideology but redirecting the present dialogue as a communal effort to achieve a goal. That goal is to enter "into the dialogue with those in prison by sharing its life-giving characteristics and identity: liberation, hope, and justice."[13]

This central theme deserves affirmation from outsiders because men incarcerated and unaware of the outcome of their future residence cling to the hope that they haven't been forgotten within a revolving world. Lastly, I considered Ray Anderson, who examines the churches' (applicable for chaplains) role of being or instead participating as an agent of reformation. There are cases where the assumption is that one insists on bringing God into the walls only to discover God is already present there. Instead, Anderson argued that the "Christian witness by their presence in the world that Christ has come to the world and has taken up the cause of the afflicted, the oppressed and the estranged as his cause. Solidarity between the community of Christian believers and the world has already been established through the incarnation."[14]

This becomes the integral point of identifying not what suffering is but what grief looks like. The bondage that the gospel message of Christ and his suffrage resembles the cause/effect model. One is tried, judged, sentenced, convicted, and depending on the outcome, will face a long grueling death at the order of their peers. No

12. Pounder, *Prison Theology*, 281.
13. Pounder, *Prison Theology*, 281.
14. Anderson, *Shape of Practical Theology*, 118.

hope exists between the sentence and the person's conviction. Thus, the cause of their consequences must be based on the reformation of that individual's human existence "of Christ as the theological ground for existence in the world and yet not of it."[15]

Those incarcerated utilize every bit of time to restructure the way they are viewed in the public's eye. The reason is the anticipation of hope for their voices to be heard and that they have sincerely become new creatures in Christ. Michelle Clifton-Soderstrom suggests that our interest should be "facing our deepest social ills, in order to advance the best that is humanity. Human flourishing participation in civic life and justice that is liberating for all and most especially for those on the margins."[16] If we as human agents carrying out the core of the gospel, it must actively be about "truth and goodness and just."[17]

We cannot discuss how we think we should fix the problem but actively formulate solutions from within the difficulty of gaining current information that is liberating. While partially the idea is to persuade the powers to set them free, the gauntlet in prison proves that every person incarcerated is not confined to an absolute evil and is exempt from being inherently good. Instead, the idea is to demonstrate God's forgiveness is unconditional and for them to seek forgiveness from those who have become victims. As much as society is disconnected from those incarcerated, they remain inherently connected as embodied people navigating a foreign terrain and must reassess their relationship with God. From a psychological perspective, it was fitting, to begin with, for current chaplains who work within the prison system.

One of them is Emily R. Brault, a state chaplain in Oregon, who affirms the idea that a person's religious belief can influence one's behavior to establish better social networks; including social bonds.[18] Furthermore, religious beliefs tend to promote self-accountability. Self-assessment would help undergird how one

15. Anderson, *Shape of Practical Theology*, 118.

16. Clifton-Soderstrom, "Liberal Arts in Prison."

17. Clifton-Soderstrom, "Liberal Arts in Prison."

18. Brault, "Pastoral Care and Counseling in Prison," 2.

would handle the traumatic experiences and the effects of their situation. While both are necessary means to tap into the psyche of one's nature, a faith-based cognitive-behavioral approach can deter one from repeating previous behaviors. To better articulate Brault's message, she believes the appropriate pastoral care model would be assessment-driven, developing a positive working relationship, assessing the stage of change, engagement of skills, and closure. She also argues that "a cursory introduction into the inmates' spiritual beliefs and cognitions will be instrumental in engaging their spirituality into the therapeutic process."[19]

Furthermore, she states that most "effective professional relationships are predicated on interpersonal skills that relay emotional congruence, warmth, accurate empathy, a judicious use of authority, and an ability to engage in healthy conflict."[20] Harold Trulear argues, "in order to truly minister to those impacted by crime and incarceration . . . must create a climate of acceptance, openness and honesty. . .where true reconciliation and redemption can occur."[21] He stresses the need that such individuals must "share their experiences, struggles, strength and hope with the congregation both in public worship and in personal interaction."[22] It must be understood that the general concept of change begins with a careful process for people to proceed through their stages and can create a positive outcome. Thus, an intervention increases the chances of establishing the will to want better, a deeper spiritual identity, and spiritual health.

Engagement skills are a necessary piece because that's where the deeper conversation helped them to navigate through their self-identity and self-narrative. From a liturgical standpoint, Jenny McBride articulates it best. She states, "The discipleship community understands the inherent social and political character of the gospel, enters new situations and creates spaces that reduce the distance between privileged and oppressed people, yearns for

19. Brault, "Pastoral Care and Counseling in Prison?" 4.
20. Brault, "Pastoral Care and Counseling in Prison?" 4.
21. Trulear, "Changing Congregational Culture," 172.
22. Trulear, "Changing Congregational Culture," 172–73.

the great reversal and enacts public repentance, performs creative nonviolent resistance to social evil and meets human need, turns toward and welcomes harsh and raw realities with compassion and courage, laments and rejects moralism, participates in Jesus' solidarity with society's victims, engages others out of a disposition of trust, and witnesses to the power of life over death and liberation over oppression."[23]

The goal was to reach for a visual and introduce an active symphony of our community beyond the walls so that those within the walls could harness a collaboration reflecting the image of an incarcerated community made in the image of God. Maria Duffy suggested that we strive "to achieve a more human presentation of the person through an integration of reason and passion."[24] Brault states it this way: "From the perspective of narrative psychology, prison conversion narratives act as a shame management and coping strategy by creating a new social identity, providing purpose and meaning to life experiences, offering empowerment as an agent of God, providing a language and framework for forgiveness and self-understanding, and allowing a sense of control over an unknown future."[25] Not knowing the uncertainty of their outcome or if freedom is in their favor, the most important thing is that some form of closure is met. This means being supportive of their social, emotional, and spiritual health. From a psychological standpoint, Browning, and Copper redirect us to B. F. Skinner's concept of behaviorism.

The idea behind this theme could also be referenced as "current forces," by which Skinner believes it's not possible to have internal mental control but being within the "environment and the reinforcements that it mediates to our responses constitute the sum of psychological realities."[26] Undoubtedly this concept can be viewed as one which should give positive reinforcement that shapes the behavior to act independently, and the reward of that

23. McBride, *Radical Discipleship*, 232–33.
24. Duffy, *Paul Ricoeur's Pedagogy of Pardon*, 23.
25. Brault, "Pastoral Care and Counseling in Prison," 7.
26. Browning and Cooper, *Religious Thought & The Modern Psychologies*, 88.

positive behavior ultimately controls itself. Skinner also puts it this way: "the behaviors classified as good or bad and right or wrong are not due to goodness or badness, or a good or bad character, or a knowledge of right and wrong; they are due to contingencies involving a great variety of reinforces, including the generalized verbal reinforces of 'Good!' 'Bad!' 'Right!' and 'Wrong!'"[27] This concept helped me with reinforcements that generated positive responses and discouraged negative ones, which is a step in the right direction. As impactful as it was, it doesn't fully answer the theological/spiritual component essential to that person's identity.

Virginia Holeman presented a more functional approach that responds to how to be present for therapeutic commitments. She laid out the following: client characteristics, therapist characteristics, dimensions of expectancy and hope, nonspecific mechanisms of change, and therapy models.[28] Generally, each functional core speaks to enhancing the client's ability to capitalize on everyday experiences, which become jointly collaborative between parties, administer hope, and address the emotional framing. This triggers the idea of utilizing cognitive reasoning and shifts one's behavior. However, the desired component is the "models of therapy."[29]

She also believes the most effective therapy relies on the client and practitioners "to remain grounded in God, seek to be open to the inspiration of the Holy Spirit, and conduct their work in a manner that is God-honoring."[30] Overall, I believe the direction of modern pastoral care is a spiritual and clinical journey that I had to incorporate into my profession as a chaplain. Certain expectations within psychology seek to control the psyche or presumably appear to influence the human dilemma, not recognizing the metaphysical (spiritual) component. However, religious leaders cannot ignore the severe medical concerns one has by making reckless and fatal mistakes regarding the mentality that one's condition is due to sin. The target is that as a professional in the field of

27. Browning and Cooper, *Religious Thought & The Modern Psychologies*, 95.
28. Holeman, *Theology for Better Counseling*, 70–77.
29. Holeman, *Theology for Better Counseling*, 76.
30. Holeman, *Theology for Better Counseling*, 77.

chaplaincy, I had to be both a Christian influencer and interfaith in incorporating my methodology and reasonably applying psychological practices when conducting pastoral care.

My obligation cannot be to seek validation for my methods but to raise questions that respond to one's faith tradition and give clarity using contemporary perspectives. One faith shapes the spiritual identity of the individual in custody. This also assists the individual in harnessing their moral compass of self-accountability and realizing how their behavior impacts their life. Using contemporary perspectives such as psychology intertwined with a spiritual component provides an abundance of reassurance to reduce anxiety and meaningful reflection. Having a socially supportive staff with access to resources that address their struggle will give a better outlook on being creative in a chaplain's response. In essence, individuals feel there's an injustice against them for their lack of awareness. They think there's a lack of care given to them which was based on a social bias too. And they've determined those biases are society's excuse not to collaborate with them and believe the compensation for their demise is to be without resources. Therefore, this must change.

OBJECTIVE, IMPLEMENTATION & STRATEGY

My objective was to incorporate and implement fundamental learning strategies through what I referred to as the 3 Cs method: caution, care, and collaboration. With this, chaplains will be more equipped to provide the proper care that's both nurturing and authentic. Caution means being alert to the conditions so that the chaplains know the person's current crisis and can provide the necessary care. Thus, planning a strategy for chaplains means observing the individuals in custody's living space (running water, the clutter of items, walls, bed set up, etc.). Furthermore, these basic needs are more than just being empathetic about their condition; they are a right to fair treatment as citizens. Acknowledging their condition raises a critical question: how can a chaplain implement some form of resolution without offending their space? And based on the resources, a chaplain will use the 3 Cs approach.

Care means locating the needs of the individuals in custody and figuring out options to provide immediate care. This is probably the essential theme for chaplains because, based on their living conditions, it has a mental and spiritual impact: the chaplain's strategy is listening to their story and essentially coaching them through their struggle. While the idea of hearing their stories without the presumption of what a chaplain might have anticipated made me even more curious about the turnout, the idea of not knowing what the outcome would have further brought me to concerns I might have overlooked. Perhaps not being aware of the caution concept pushed me to the framework of what I, as a chaplain, consciously or unconsciously ignored.

When it comes to the strategy behind care, the motive is to gain insight into how their care becomes critical. An example of how this strategy is envisioned would be caring for an indigent individual who is trying to obtain religious materials. While this item seems small, the goal was trying to discover if the smallest amount of care, as simple as a bible or other religious materials, would be equally as sufficient for them to feel heard. Care isn't always about discussion or encouraging words. Sometimes the most significant impact to help change someone's perspective comes in small acts of kindness and compassion.

The final strategy is the collaborative approach, which comes from the active willingness to be mutually cooperative and accountable for one's actions. This means first realizing the chaplain needs feedback from the individual in custody regarding how one's influence will assist them during their incarceration. Secondly, being collaborative also means recognizing the limitations both parties have and making the necessary adjustments to fulfill the expectations. These limitations are not to make promises or guarantee blindly that an individual will receive. If in doubt something might not be fulfilled, it's best to find an alternative that you can guide them with other options. Collaboration is working alongside them to help the individual in custody resolve the crisis so that it has a long-term positive effect on their overall well-being.

To make this possible, I had to assess how I was working with individuals in custody and know the best time when to refer to the other professionals in situations that were beyond my ability. Considering individuals in custody are classified as a protected group, I adjusted my surveys for persons formerly incarcerated to bring to light themes they would have liked to see from chaplains. Furthermore, a survey was drafted for them to respond based on the experience and limitations they felt prevented them from getting the pastoral care they needed. Another strategy I conducted was a six-week post-survey with chaplains after we collectively reviewed the responses from the formerly incarcerated that focus on the 3 Cs: caution, care, and collaboration.

The questions directed toward the former incarcerated individuals were: How effective was the pastoral care you received while incarcerated? In what specific ways was the pastoral care you received helpful? In what particular ways was the pastoral care you received from chaplains in prison not helpful? If some of your pastoral care needs were met to some degree in prison, how did that show up in your everyday life? What feedback would you give to chaplains that provided care to better serve people currently residing? What resources have you found helpful when you've collaborated with a chaplain on your spiritual journey? What should chaplains be made aware of when providing care to those incarcerated? Moving forward, what would you like to see more of from chaplaincy? Each of these questions demonstrates concerns when assessing chaplaincy in prison.

Some of those responses mainly addressed obtaining resources to better equip the individuals in custody based on either being upon re-entry back into society or themes that provided the education they didn't acquire when they were free. Also, knowing that individuals in custody needed consistency, giving space to examine their spiritual journey. With that comes the responsibility of not limiting them based on their incarceration but would further assist in their development of care for the future. This would further suggest that

I provide them with opportunities for reassurance within their religious community and that prevention systems become the norm. Ideally, the chaplains had to concentrate on what type of spiritual programming one could achieve and feel welcomed.

In light of these questions, theologically, the merger of one's humanness and spirituality become that person's moment to establish divine humility. To clarify, divine humility means when one embraces the image of being created as God intended and willingly faces every encounter, one has to become intentional about being subservient to the *Soli Deo Gloria* (glory to God alone). This brings the assurance of hope, justice, love, and forgiveness. Furthermore, it becomes the new way for propagating determination for the individual and discovering a methodology that displays the function they internally strive to achieve. Perhaps the best approach is to recognize that prison theology is contextual theology, which means the conversations must address the immediate and future needs of that individual.

In other words, men that are incarcerated are in a constant move of shifting from a perceived challenging behavior to a progressive state. While it's essential to know and understand the effectiveness of pastoral care, I had to consult other chaplains working in the prison system, which reflected on their ministry as caregivers and how they impacted those they served. How has the pastoral care you provided been most effective to those incarcerated? Why? What evidence do you have that your caregiving was effective? What methods have you used to obtain feedback from those in your care, and what feedback did you receive from the care receivers? What do incarcerated care receivers expect from you as a prison chaplain? Moving forward, what would you like to see more of from chaplaincy? In retrospect, this shift will require that the community at large recognize that through the eyes of God they are also a part of the people of God. It's our responsibility to acknowledge their humanity in the church when the larger community outside of the church doesn't. Even as one reflects on the traumatic experience based on the crime against them, God's unfailing love has not ceased for the incarcerated person.

Therefore, any preconceived notions or concerns I presumed they needed became an urgency to allow them to tell their own story and not measure how their past behaviors would impact their future. The consensus was that they did not receive the opportunity to address their traumatic experiences, and the reaction to their demise was a response desiring to gain attention. No matter how unreasonable it was, instead, it was a cry for help, and when guidance wasn't available, they leaned on the tactics of how to survive that best suited their immediate needs. This reality was my awareness of people in custody having psychological and spiritual damage that inflamed an opposition for them to utilize their role in the world as we know it. When one is accustomed to tantalizing any possibility to attain success, it inevitably becomes part of that person's character.

As a result, I had to find ways of redirecting them to a place of imagining what they would want to learn about themselves and how they would like to be treated as human beings. In that environment, they've been accustomed to being treated with punitive measures. Considering they've been traumatized, the objective became searching for their own identity and taking a moment to reflect constructively without all of the negative distractions. By acknowledging their predicament, the initiative became outlining what they felt would put them in a position to reach their own goal of mental and spiritual health. Furthermore, by identifying opportunities they could quickly enter and programs with particular requirements before entry, one could participate in programs that would help them develop their strengths.

These sessions imply that one must be empathetic enough to allow one to forge a newness that ultimately validates them as a person broken and working towards being whole. At the same time, they've come to the reality that one must not willfully continue keeping the trauma alive to disrupt, dismantle, debilitate, and diminish who they are. They are not their traumatic experiences, but they are the victims of a community that has failed to provide the necessary resources to prevent those traumatic experiences. Thus, accountability comes with an assurance of hopefulness that they will amount to something greater than anticipated. Along with that, the implication is if one witnesses a better and more secure alternative one will benefit from, others will be motivated to acquire the steps of transformation for themselves.

Therefore, the 3 Cs were put into practice with each chaplain (including myself) and focused on applying them to individuals in custody within a concentrated area. Once completed, we compared our results based on the information given. Within my context, I used an area known as "restricted housing," where I would meet with individuals who have received disciplinary actions based on the findings from the disciplinary committee. In these cases, the individuals were given the option to participate in the session or opt-out. This setting using the 3 Cs pushed me to figure out what I missed or overlooked, what wasn't being addressed, what immediate care was most pertinent to them, how the lack of care impacted them, when was the care they needed most influential during their time being incarcerated, as a chaplain where did they need me the most to advocate for them, and most importantly, how could I help them obtain it.

Implementation

WITHIN MY DATA ANALYSIS, the result of my chaplaincy training brought attention to themes chaplains had not considered initially regarding the pivotal role they played. Often there was a general observation (figure out what was needed and deliver a remedy) without recognizing their current predicament. Caution was more focused on paying attention to what immediate care was most needed. Care, at one point, was attending to duty instead of showing empathy and the love of performing ministry at work. Thus, collaborative efforts were to give them an interpretative alternative they could work through independently. This type of framework was necessary to abolish because it didn't adhere to the spiritual care the individual in custody deserved.

Therefore, implementing the 3 Cs concept became a fundamental method that was sincere and captivating to relinquish the systemic ideology of one's view of those incarcerated. Also, within my observation, chaplains working in prison were diverse and theologically open to various beliefs, and despite their core beliefs, they were applying my methodology to multiple religions. Thus, my concept became a success because it serves as a guide for them through working with a multifaceted population of people having diverse backgrounds and personalities. Implementing the 3 Cs gave clarity to unexpected encounters one may have. It also generated further conversation for both parties to learn from one another and how their interests met.

One example was a chaplain trying to understand what type of dilemma an individual in custody faced by first assessing the external environment. When it came to caring, the chaplain needed to understand their story first and determine what care could be properly given. Moreover, the collaborative measure set the way to assure the individual in custody that the chaplain was holding themselves accountable for the action they intended to perform. This also means the individual senses that they are a priority and not a burden. Furthermore, collaboration means the chaplain tries to make sure their needs are met to recognize their worth. And having a strategy within the intro of the engagement meant the same method was applied, but alternatives to how they were carried out were subject the change.

EFFECTS OF VIOLENCE ON THE INCARCERATED

Before getting into the implementation, I wanted to address the importance of prison chaplaincy. Post-COVID in a maximum-security prison had been a cumbersome, stressful, and grueling time period to navigate for the individuals in custody as well as staff. Even as the institution was on the cusp of bringing individuals back into the institution, most of the men incarcerated have not seen their family or friends. In fact, during the beginning of COVID in March of 2020 up until now, several men did not get the chance to say goodbye to their loved ones. Roughly thirty men (maybe more) have passed as a result of contracting COVID, and the rise of another variant makes the expectancy of reintroducing religious services to those incarcerated much more complex. Perhaps the greater issue that men will face is being unable to have physical interactions with someone outside of the prison system, which includes family and friends that support them.

Emotional, spiritual, and physical trauma impacts incarcerated men to the degree it takes a drastic toll on their mental capacity to cope with the reality of prison life. Oftentimes men that have extensively long sentences are found to abuse psychotropic medications to combat the stringent reality of the prison. This is a result of not finding healthy ways to cognitively demonstrate the desire to change and giving up hope that they have the capacity to change. This idea of change isn't so much having a different approach to life but more so the idea of wanting to live. Perhaps some would call it survival, but in retrospect it's much more volatile than that.

The focus should be on resolving critical issues incarcerated men face to survey a consensus to evaluate using questions that point towards a trajectory which encompasses their internal concerns: emotional, spiritual, and psychological trauma. I believe here's where chaplains come into play, because we become the person that humanizes them and assists to provide a comprehensive care that only seeks the well-being of that individual. We become that compassionate caregiver that provides some form of stability and balance during unbearable times of despair. We become the instrument they will utilize to formulate their own opinion of the larger society that some care enough about them to see them live on.

We become the tangible evidence that they are not forgotten and whatever reasonable chance to equip them to move forward, we as chaplains become that to them. With the ways in which the individuals in custody have anxiety about incarceration, medical issues they had prior to their incarceration or other circumstances they've mitigated has now become something beyond their control. This creates an unsettling mental state to ascertain, and that's where chaplains need to become more aware of when providing care. However, I believe, at times our biases create a certain proclivity subconsciously about those incarcerated.

It is either from the personal matter that's identical to the individual in custody's crime or the knowing of someone else who has been a victim of a similar crime. It's natural to have some reservations or a reluctance to express some form of empathy towards those that have negatively impacted our community. To face that bias, we begin to exhibit godly grace within ourselves to influence potential long-term change and we reserve room for a godly causative response in their spiritual journey. Because the duty is to maintain the integrity of what pastoral care should look like, we must as chaplains remain consistent to administer care and intentionally compromise our biases to ensure their care is met. I want to be clear that this doesn't mean your compromising your reaction but compromising the inception of allowing those biases to dictate if you should administer care.

Care should always be unbiased and fair. Chaplains are human beings as well, and they feel emotional over tragedies that impact their personal livelihoods. Thus, a chaplain has to embrace every encounter with individuals in custody as a way to practice blind forgiveness. When I suggest blind forgiveness means whether one knows the details of what caused them to become incarcerated or not, we must view them as children of God needing comfort. It's not a chaplain's role to judge, denigrate, or demonize because of an unfortunate choice one has made.

Our role as chaplains is to get the individual in custody to reimagine what freedom looks like internally in order to properly combat the external conditions they reside in. Therefore, to provide a bit more background to my case study, it is based on an experience I've encountered when I had to provide care to someone dealing with trauma. For the sake of confidentiality, I will refer to the gentleman as "BJ." BJ was sentenced to four years for carjacking and armed robbery. He was brought to the institution for be an "absconder" (failure to report to his parole agent) for six months. As a result, he has to spend the remaining time of his parole incarcerated. During this time, BJ receives a call from family members that his brother was shot a killed at a family and friends' event near his neighborhood.

BJ was heartbroken and devastated. Out of his six siblings (four boys and two girls), two of his brothers were killed due to gun violence, and his older brother was now killed due to gun violence, which means his mother will now have to bury her third son, and BJ, being the youngest male, was incarcerated. Due to COVID restrictions, he is unable to attend his brother's funeral physically and can't comfort his family members as he would wish. His only alternative is via Zoom. He can't communicate with his family and is only allowed to view the body of his brother.

Implementation

Devastated by this arrangement, he looks to chaplaincy for some form of awareness, care, and understanding. In most cases, mental health professionals and chaplains are made aware of crises individuals in custody face. His biggest desolation is not so much being incarcerated but being incarcerated at the time of a loved one's death. In most cases, similar to this one, the necessity is to provide assurance of hope and tranquility that works for him. His brother being violently taken away makes his time of incarceration a much more arduous process. The idea is to cautiously approach his vulnerability in search of measuring what care is needed and what I can provide that speaks specifically to his vicissitude.

As a result, I will address the issues utilizing a concept I've created called the 3 Cs: caution, care, and collaboration. This is a suitable methodology because it deals with him realizing his current situation has made him limited in what he can do. Also, it gives the chaplain a chance to recognize externally how he was affected and how he is responding to outsiders. Thus, as a chaplain he needs assistance to resist the re-traumatizing news of his deceased brother to negatively impact his time of incarceration. Instead, the mission is to take a collaborative effort that supports BJ's overall experience: he is not alone, and he is cared for during his time of incarceration.

The reason this is vital is due to the environment he's in, the traumatic experience of being limited to provide care to his family and working with him adjusting to the reality of a lost one. Considering this was the first time he lost a relative while incarcerated, I used these accounts as ways to reduce recidivism. In most cases, individuals like BJ are forever reminded that prison is the worst place to be in, and being absent from your family is one thing those incarcerated regret. Therefore, I will provide a brief transcript and then transition into the logistics of what sources I used to assist me in providing pastoral care in relation to his trauma.

THE CASE STUDY

For privacy purposes, I've altered specifics to protect the privacy of the individual in custody. The beginning of this event took place via phone, where I received a call from the counselor to come and check on BJ during a funeral visit. Prior to coming to the funeral via Zoom, his demeanor was melancholy and anxious. With little time to prep and reading that his religious affiliation was Christian, I grabbed as much material as he would be allowed to take back to his cell. To properly envision how this narrative speaks of trauma and the ways in which I provided pastoral care, I will provide a concise transcript based on the encounter I had with BJ.

BJ: (violently screaming and pounding his fist on the table profusely, while looking via Zoom at his deceased brother)

Counselor A: (sees chaplain from afar and motions hand, inviting them into the Zoom funeral)

Chaplain Davis: I just got the call that he requested me and heard a scream. Was that BJ?

Counselor A: Yes, and I'm afraid he's taking it pretty hard.

(counselor steps out and Chaplain Davis observes the Zoom funeral with BJ, while waiting for it to end)

Chaplain Davis: Hey BJ, I'm so sorry for your loss. Is there anything I can do?

BJ: I don't know right now. They f***ing killed my brother, chap! God, where were you? Now, my mom only has one son left. (Tears falling uncontrollably) This s*** hurt, chap ,and I can't do nothin'.

Chaplain Davis: BJ, I want you to try something with me. Take a deep breath. Take a few more. Very good. I know this is a hard time, but you caught a blessing, brother. You got a chance to see your brother one more time.

BJ: Yeah, but my family needs me.

Chaplain Davis: They do need you and they will always need you. Now, you must be the voice of reason to your family to keep on living. They are counting on you to come home. They are waiting for you.

BJ: Yeah, I know. So, what do I do now?

Chaplain Davis: Call them and tell them I love you. Tell them you're done with prison and work on rebuilding your relationship with your mother and your kids.

BJ: Thanks, Chap. Can you do something for me? Can you pray for me?

Chaplain Davis: Of course. Dear God, I thank you here for brother BJ. He's at a place where he's unsure of how to proceed in life. This is a difficult time for BJ, but God, I trust you that you will place your loving arms around BJ and his family. God, I pray that he leans on you for peace that surpasses all understanding and hands dry his tears. God be with BJ during this time. All these things we pray in Jesus' name, amen.

BJ: Thanks, chap, for just being here. I really appreciate it.

Chaplain Davis: (Nod of gratitude) You're more than welcome; I'll stop by and check on you. God bless you brother and sorry for your loss.

EXAMINATION

The brief glimpse of BJ's reality is the sensation of not only viewing the traumatic experience of his deceased brother but the idea of trying to sustain a sense of reality being incarcerated. What BJ needed at that moment was the presence of someone who could genuinely empathize his challenging circumstance. The other awareness that I needed to keep in mind was that considering his incarceration, he was feeling overwhelmed, enraged, ashamed and perhaps just wanted to collapse. However, I had to keep in mind something from Bessel Van Der Kolk. He says that we approach with an open heart to help them find " (1) a way to become calm and focused, (2) learning to maintain that calm response to images, thoughts, sounds, or physical sensations that remind you of the past, (3) finding a way to be fully alive in the present and engaged with the people around you, (4) not having to keep secrets from yourself, including secrets about the ways that you have managed to survive."[1] Furthermore, it's likely that BJ's childhood memories have now been shattered because that physical relationship with his brother has been torn.

The idea of him one day returning to society causes him to have fears that will attempt to hijack his thoughts. BJ is vulnerable, enraged, and looking for any form of resolution for his trauma. Kolk suggest that "change begins when we learn to 'own' our emotional brains. That means learning to observe and tolerate the heartbreaking and gut-wrenching sensations that register misery and humiliation."[2] We can't simply dismiss the instant reaction to one's tragedy but allow them to embrace the helplessness and being available to give them the care they need. What should be understood is that this methodology can be used as a substitute for cognitive therapy and, inclusive of other approaches, can be used to assist those dealing with trauma.

However, this approach positively interacts with the 3 Cs concept I've introduced. The first C is caution. Caution is becoming aware of the activity taking place and circumstances that impact the person's traumatic experience—also, observing the reactions to what creates a traumatic experience. In BJ's case, it is him handcuffed at his hands and ankles, while viewing his deceased brother's funeral. Unfortunately, he is unable to speak to his family.

So, naturally he is distraught about being incarcerated and still trying to process the ghastly circumstance as well as his own limitation. Thus, by paying attention to his physical inability to move freely and not being able to provide sufficient comfort to his family, the focus would be to apprehend his desire to concentrate

1. Van Der Kolk, *Body Keeps the Score*, 205–6.
2. Van Der Kolk, *Body Keeps the Score*, 131.

on his own livelihood. Also, with care is insisting on shifting the atmosphere to become as therapeutic for that moment and redistributing his energy to a place of peaceful solitude. While being present, it's at the moment he knows his care is high priority and "to be" along with them in their quietness is all that matters. This stems from Paul's idea that "we are troubled on every side, yet not distressed; we are perplexed, but not in despair."[3]

Along with that, his transition to leaving prison was slowly approaching six months and yet he would have to face the reality that his brother was taken from him as well as his family. By approaching with caution, we become aware regarding how to be sensitive and observant to the atmosphere which we enter into. Furthermore, by having the intentions to only address his internal care is what further influences beneficial pastoral care. When it comes to care, here's where the tipping point begins of transforming and developing the spiritual thrust of what godly peace looks like. It's common for those incarcerated to use a negative antidote to reinforce the despair and entertain some extreme form of cynical acts as a reaction to the altered reality they exist in.

However, as a caregiver it's our duty to rightfully give them a glimpse of the gospel or a type of Christ-like response. The goal to shift BJ's current vision of the universe into a fresher glimpse of what God desires and how God inordinately will not rest until which what is upside down is turned right side up.[4] Essentially, to provide care is to actively alter perception that care exists, and BJ's perception of care was that very little compassion would be given taking into consideration of the mental climate of the institution. Thus, I had to find a way to assist BJ with the reality of being incarcerated and the inability of being able to respond to family. One major piece that was apparent is a statement made by Shelly Rambo suggest that what BJ is facing was the "afterlife of the cross."

She also argues "there is no clear-cut line separating the two: life is not a departure from death but, instead, a different

3. 2 Cor 4:8.
4. Tisdale, *Prophetic Preaching*, 37.

relationship to death and life."[5] The coping mechanism to mentally and spiritual make an adjustment was the complexity of BJ trying to make sense of outcome. Rambo also suggest that "there is no clear-cut line separating the two; life is not a departure from death but, instead, a different relationship to death and life."[6] Furthermore, care needed to be provided to BJ's to address the wounds of his guilt of being absent. Thus, the redirection would be to steer him into reality away from guilt and more towards an expansive vision of what his life can look like.

One thing I know is significant to providing care is considering how this experience will affect his life. This experience has created a gap between what he hoped for and the experience of what he's dealing with. Ideally, BJ expected to return home with the expectation of rekindling the past with family and friends, in this case his brother. His brother was his last oldest brother who supported him, remained in contact with him during his sentence and provided for his children when they were in need. But now there was trauma gap that Harold Dean Trulear states: that "there's a gap between expectations and experience."[7] I had to use this moment to revise this experience into something more.

Being incarcerated, one is accustomed to being in a cell having anti-social thinking and anti-social companions, instead of having prosocial thinking and prosocial companionship. Instead, for those incarcerated and those involved in providing care, we must approach their experience with healing restoration. Though he was incarcerated, BJ looked forward to indulging with his brother prior to his incarceration. Thus, Trulear believes that we must use new language, new ways of thinking, create new paradigms and climates that are welcoming.[8] Within that climate there must be an inclusion that reduces the stigma and shame.[9] Trulear puts it this way as far as dealing with the gap between expectation

5. Rambo, *Resurrecting Wounds*, 7.
6. Rambo, *Resurrecting Wounds*, 7.
7. Trulear, "Loving the Incarcerated."
8. Trulear, "Loving the Incarcerated."
9. Trulear, "Loving the Incarcerated."

and experience: "because of the early release of the convict (Jesus), you get early release from your habits, from your sickness, from your trouble. How do you deal with that gap between expectation and experience? Through the strength of the ex-con who died for your sins."[10] BJ needed to be reminded that through his experience, he needed to replace his vulnerability with God's strength to heal his wounded spirit.

What must be understood is that wounds are often depicted as a human weakness, and through traumatic experiences, ideally the preference would be to erase the unaccommodated human limitation. However, Shelly Rambo's goal based off the cross is to redefine a more expansive vision of the human understanding of trauma.[11] In light of resurfacing wounds, one must insist on exposing insidious practices that have been ongoing specifically to Black communities who have suffered from what she calls "insidious trauma." She also states that "insidious trauma was not trauma isolated to an event but a continuing series of events that compromised the conditions of ongoing life."[12] Thus, the difficulty was to not entertain horrific events but to reflect that his own life is constant resurrection, that he can continue to live through the complexities of life.

By internally having the impulse to overcome, facing his trauma, and working toward healing the old wound of the past family history, he begins to transmit an idea of emerging from that turmoil a different sacred story. That sacred story is creating another path that leads to ongoing affirmation of self-reflection and spiritual awareness that one's life matters to the community at large. We've understood that approaching with caution are the ways in which we are aware of the physical plight of a person's living conditions, understand the impact of how the physical plight affects the mental state, and how the mental state disrupts spiritual direction of the individual. When it comes to care, we realize that care is the critical point of transmitting the need and genuinely

10. Trulear, "Loving the Incarcerated."
11. Rambo, *Resurrecting Wounds*, 33.
12. Rambo, *Resurrecting Wounds*, 78.

discovering the ways in which one is positively impacting to their future. However, when it comes to collaboration is the point of actively participating in illustrating how their physical plight becomes and the measure of care received redefines their internal as well as external outcome of their future.

Collaboration is to actively participate in the reconstruction of their demise and strategize what their outcome of continuous care become. The idea is an inception of hope and rediscovering their faith through circumstances out of their control. Virginia Todd Holeman, when approaching with a therapeutic characteristic that one address a specific aspect when providing care and contributing ways of creating to healthy relationships that present positive outcomes,[13] states, "an emotionally and socially intelligent counselor will build stronger connections with clients than those unfortunate counselors who fall short in these areas. Skillful counselors will match their method of engagement to the client instead of expecting the client to fit the counselor."[14]

The only way a chaplain would be able to effectively engage with BJ is to vocally and physically inform them they are not alone. While some methodologies approach trauma with specific mechanisms of change, Holeman argues that they should be nonspecific and address three ideas: their emotional regulation, cognitive reframing, and behavioral shifts.[15] For this reason, collaboration becomes the end result to being cautious and providing care, mainly because it is an interplay of inspiring an external and internal hope that with his family healing begins. Real healing is therapeutic, and when it's successful, it deepens one's theological reflection on how they view God's activity and where they see themselves in that concept.

Holeman puts it this way: "Provided that theologically reflective practitioners remain grounded in God, seek to be open to the inspiration of the Holy Spirit, and conduct their work in a manner that is God-honoring, client-respecting and ethically appropriate, then the Holy Spirit can do what the Holy Spirit does best—help

13. Holeman, *Theology for Better Counseling*, 72.
14. Holeman, *Theology for Better Counseling*, 72.
15. Holeman, *Theology for Better Counseling*, 76.

people more fully embody the image of God in their daily lives."[16] Thus, the goal of collaboration is to make one feel he's safe, being prepared to provide proper referrals of care beyond my capacity and being readily available for any emotional (including behavioral) regulation that brings one to state of equilibrium.[17] Collaboration provides one an extra layer of protection and allowing an opportunity to spiritually cope with one's traumatic experience. The role of a chaplain is to not only provide space but ideally making that space sacred. When a person is incarcerated, security and safety must extend to the person's overall well-being.

Thus, it includes working alongside them to face the trauma and ensuring that their perception of care is authentic. By being attentive to their surroundings, a chaplain has the capacity to shift negative atmosphere echoing the lamentations of that individual to God. Furthermore, collaboration acts as a guide toward healing future trauma. Menakem states that as much as one is being pulled back and forth between time, is to remember these are opposing forces.[18] Menakem states, "the first is your body's natural urge to settle and relax. The second is your body's equally natural urge to protect itself. This can manifest as activation, an urge to move."[19]

By allowing the movement of one's emotions to metabolize the events and paying attention to how one's body responds to opposition, one learns to navigate through trauma that bends towards self-care. From what I gathered trauma is under-internalized and becomes a reactional response that mirrors the "dirty pain," which means one is in conflict in their implicit bias as well as attempting to regulate the abnormal circumstances they face.[20] When we bend towards care, we give practice to self-love of our minds, body, and spirit. BJ was already disconnected from family; he needed a cautious caring collaborative approach intertwined. Furthermore, if

---

16. Holeman, *Theology for Better Counseling*, 77.

17. Holeman, *Theology for Better Counseling*, 169.

18. Resmaa Menakem, *My Grandmother's Hands*, 179.

19. Resmaa Menakem, *My Grandmother's Hands*, 179.

20. Resmaa Menakem, *My Grandmother's Hands*, 167.

one is unable to provide comforting care to their family, the chaplain has the capacity to inspire one to care for themselves.

EVALUATION

As I reflect on my work, I understood the importance of what healing of those incarcerated should look like and how my role as a chaplain plays an integral part to give a sense of sacredness. While psychology helps relief some of the anxiety one may have or various treatments that assist in suppressing the entanglement of a memory, spiritual care grants one the permission to enter a space with their religious affiliation. Mental health is much more than giving access to a physical antidote to combat the ills of this world but arriving at a form of spiritual enlightenment that develops into a peace that can surpass all carnal understanding. When one has positive reinforcement surrounding them, one can shift the external conditions into an opportunity of pursing intimacy with God.

Also, it gives the person a chance to become intimate with themselves and all the challenges one has. By learning a methodology from other authors, I thought there should be a concise example of how to address those incarcerated and the caliber of people prison chaplains come across. As a result, the 3 Cs method emerged: caution, care, and collaboration. The reason these were chosen was taking into consideration the environment of the prison. Every initial engagement is always predicated on the social location that affects the individual in custody.

Staying alert and attentive to those we provide care to always has the potential to affect the ways in which chaplains respond to various crises. From that, care becomes the focal point of learning the best alternative to impact those incarcerated and how we as chaplains journey with them through their situation. Lastly, collaboration becomes the instrument used to fortify the soul from negative ideas of despair and promote long-term hope for the individual. Chaplaincy in the prison is an ongoing learning experience. I can't expect to get every encounter right or my assistance will inevitably change one's life instantly.

Life does not work like that, and with most men (or women) incarcerated for long-term sentences, chaplains or those ministering in the prison system need to adjust their scope of their life as another chance to rekindle hope, another chance to reevaluate their place in the world and their relationship with God. Laying aside any perspective that they are not exempt from the grace of God, while facing trauma they understand God is much closer to their healing process than anticipated. Therefore, my desire is that I have learned to be empathetic to those incarcerated and that chaplains examine closely how they provide care only then will be able to bring a refreshing spirit to the dark places in people's lives. With the assurance of hope, all things are possible to face when one is confronted with trauma.

DATA GATHERING & ANALYSIS PLAN

The change made within delivery (not the 3 Cs concept) was how the chaplain approached the individual in custody. It's important to note that some changes are contingent on how the individual in custody views chaplains or other persons that act as caregivers in the facility. Another change was to recognize the limited pro-social engagements the individual in custody has. The difference in the chaplains' approach was the individuals in custody lacked spiritual attention. If the person doesn't have a religious background or has a bias toward any religious affiliate, then the chaplain would have to approach them with a humanistic awareness to help guide them through values that interest them. Furthermore, chaplains had to shift into the role the person needed at that moment. This means connecting with what will motivate them the most to examine how they view their future.

The following questions were directed toward formerly incarcerated persons shedding light on pastoral care's presence in prison or lack thereof.

How effective was the pastoral care you received while incarcerated? In what specific ways was the pastoral care you received helpful? In what specific ways was the pastoral care you received from chaplains in prison not helpful? *Out of eight participants, most stated that chaplains often provided pastoral care during times of need. How they offered care was one-on-one engagement through prayer and conducting classes that would promote spiritual development. However, the way they weren't effective was by doing the bare minimum, which consisted of not advocating enough for them. Some chaplains were there to be seen and not present during their crisis. They were there simply for employment and didn't take the ministry of chaplaincy seriously. While very few provided one-on-one pastoral care, other chaplains were passively biased toward cultural differences, mainly toward people of color. By not integrating care for all, they would focus only on a particular group of people that were like-minded.*

This question indicates a theme of the inconsistency of pastoral care given to them during their incarceration. While having some engagement is sufficient for the moment, long term the absence of chaplains profoundly impacts the core of their emotional and spiritual health. An additional theme is being empathetic to everyone, which challenges the chaplains to the implicit bias one has toward individuals in custody. The chaplain's role is more than creating normalcy in a stressful environment; but mirrors the faith which we represent. We chaplains represent the sacred fundamentals of human-to-human tranquility and must have the flexibility of bringing something transcendental in every approach. Without that experience, we knowingly and unknowingly do more harm than good.

If some of your pastoral care needs were met to some degree in prison, how did that show up in your everyday life? *Out of eight participants, six agreed that chaplains would help refer them to services once released. They also assisted them in getting educational programming. However, two participants suggested they weren't provided the necessary resources to accommodate their spiritual needs.*

Furthermore, all eight participants stated that lackluster engagement from chaplains or the allotted time to be given pastoral care gave them more time to reflect on their consequences and discover their faith related to what others might be going through.

This question posed to them indicates a theme of resources. The main reason resources are pivotal to those in custody focuses on those trying to obtain education and literature. Not knowing what individuals in custody have caused them to become indigent prevents them from getting access to specific literature that could further motivate them to positive change. While some have little to no expectation of chaplains being evolved in their affairs, in retrospect, it would cause two possible posing themes. Either one, they will resort to searching for all positive reinforcements to engage with, or they will engage in unconstructed engagements to negatively affect their future during incarceration. **Thus, chaplains must advocate for them to obtain resources and assist in enhancing their outcomes for the future.**

What feedback would you give to chaplains that provide care to better serve people currently residing in the prison? *All eight participants believe that chaplains could be better by being consistent with everyone, being available, being present, and most importantly, showing love and compassion to every individual. It's much more than facilitating a Sunday service but exemplifying relational trust that extends to those incarcerated daily.*

This question posed to them indicates the level of care. In most cases, chaplains are religious coordinators of various religions in prison. However, chaplains are expected to be versatile in the absence of an individual in custody whose religious affiliate isn't present. Thus, prompting the chaplain to conduct a service as if they provide a sacred space for those in custody. **While some may find this engagement conflicting with one's faith, what must be understood is that a chaplain is not compromising one's faith but providing the ability to adapt to the environment for collaboration purposes. By having space available for those** individuals, one further encourages community enrichment, not just for some but for all.

What resources have you found helpful when you've collaborated with a chaplain on your spiritual journey? *All eight participants agreed fellowship with the chaplain was essential to collaboratively. One suggested even further that "we are not forgotten." Further states were coming together with individuals in custody that "what it takes to endure our sentences, rejecting the shame." The focus became relying on collaboration and pastoral care from one chaplain to providing pastoral care one another. If the same idea were transactional from the chaplains to those incarcerated, one could positively change someone's life.*

This question posed to them indicates a theme of a spiritual journey. One of Jesus' requirements was that our presence be authentic. This reminds me of the movie *When They See Us.* **The project model included various elements of developing a workable praxis; the spiritual component must show up in ways the person will feel the chaplain's presence. This is important because we are the physical representation of God! To those we serve, chaplains become the incarnate display of God's grace and mercy given to them. Moreover, through their misfortune, we should act as agents of compassion and integrity.**

What should chaplains be made aware of when providing care to those incarcerated? *Most of them agreed to be ready to deal with anything. Either emotional, spiritual, mental, or disability, one may learn to be patient with them. Also, chaplains are accountable to the community; they provide service that affects them inside and outside the prison. Thus, while being cautious with the service they provide, they must also realize they're dealing with a vulnerable population of people trying not to keep their composure to the shocking reality of being in prison.*

This question posed to them indicates a theme of awareness. Individuals in custody have different ways of adapting to prison. While most find prison a traumatic experience, others struggle with being wholly separated from loved ones—even the idea of losing a loved one while in custody triggers different reactions to the prison environment. **Even how to engage with one's mental, spiritual, and emotional capacity to cognitively understand must be considered. Thus, every individual must be treated with the utmost respect. Being protective of their vulnerability establishes trust, which ensures that a chaplain is being authentic and consistent.**

Moving forward, what would you like to see more of from chaplaincy? *All eight participants stated they wanted to see the external church provide reentry and care for families of the incarcerated. Better standards and compensation for prisons, empowering residents, better training such as clinical pastoral education implemented, reminding they are people with families that care about their wellbeing, accepting the task as being the resources to other venues to assist them during and after their release.*

This question posed to them indicates a theme of community involvement. It's been the idea that churches or religious organizations come into the prison to assist in providing religious services. However, on a grander scale, individuals in custody seek more than just pastoral care but aftercare services provided to them once released from prison. **Some religious organizations may not have the capacity to operate independently, so working with like-minded persons that aspire to reduce recidivism becomes equally essential between the individual in custody and the community at large. Furthermore, consistent training for chaplains about how they deal with the evolving population we service and work alongside those who desire the same positive outcome. This is revealed in the training that often chaplains have a closed interpretation regarding what one assumes will work for the individual in custody, rather than offering an option for the individual to choose what alternative best fits them.**

EVALUATION & LEARNING

Upon my discovery, the method of addressing tangible things wasn't sufficient. The individuals in custody need to be surrounded by the components that could mentally and physically participate in functions that promote their spiritual care. For any religious affiliation, including the church or person considering becoming a chaplain in prison, it should be noted they are dealing with a sensitive context of persons that are deserving of care. Set aside any bias, the gravity of the depth of trauma one faces pre- or post-incarceration must be able to enter in with a particular mission that translates into the parameters of the population they serve.

This triune expression recognizes the foci while enabling the person multiple ways of working toward a common goal and not self-gratification. Prison ministry is equal to, if not more important than, a parish setting because it is a call to minister to those disenfranchised. It is a call that doesn't politically, socially, or spiritually receive monetary assistance. But what it does is motivate us to respond to the ills of this world and come face to face with those impacted by it. Thus, the church is not a building but a collective movement of people aspiring to reflect the image of God and how to serve the least of these.

Consensus of 3 Cs Findings

Using the 3 Cs methodology, I used similar questions asked in the survey for the chaplains. This time the application of the 3 Cs methodology was conducted.[1]

How has the pastoral care you provided been most effective to those incarcerated? Why? The most effective pastoral care I have provided to those incarcerated involves a ministry of presence. Being and remaining physically present in an environment formed deeply by mistrust is often the most healing and caring act in which I can engage. It begins with the mindset. If, as chaplains or pastoral caregivers in carceral spaces, we see those we are serving in the same way, most of society does, as depraved, unworthy, and evil, in need of us to save, rescue, or bring "God" to them, we will never indeed provide pastoral care. My act of first seeing an incarcerated individual as a whole person created in the image of God is what has allowed me to be trusted to provide care and to be able to enter the deeper spaces that need healing.

---

1. Note: Some of the participants opted out of the project due to unforeseen circumstances, which resulted in me only using five participants and key elements I felt addressed the new methodology.

What evidence do you have that your caregiving was effective? Something about the art of storytelling allows them to transmit a form of being on sacred ground where they are unashamed. In those moments of care, I tell them, "Permit yourself to cry. No need to feel restricted here. I am with you." Words of comfort and protection offer them an outlet of reassurance they are not left behind. In those moments, they need to know they have not been forgotten by society. They need and want to know they aren't remembered as a criminal but recognized as an individual with emotions, feelings, and trauma seeking healing from untethered resources.

What methods have you used to obtain feedback from those in your care, and what feedback did you receive from the care receivers? Closed-ended questions like: "What about our visit today was helpful for you?" "You just shared a lot of information about your mom; what will you miss about her the most?" I have received feedback that calling people to my office was worrisome. They had to wait all night, wondering what we would talk about (call passes distributed the night before). I have also had people tell me they do not want to speak to a chaplain. That is okay. I honored their request and tried to let them know they were not alone if they ever needed someone to talk to.

What methods have you used when you've collaborated with an individual in custody's spiritual journey? By having the willingness of the individual in custody to express emotions not typically expressed. Individuals in custody do not cry, as part of my experience, and attempt to control their heartfelt feelings. During grief care, individuals in custody have stated that they appreciated being called into spaces where they are allowed to grieve even for a moment, such as the major's office, a classroom with an officer, or the housing unit counseling office, and the movement of other individuals in the central desk area is restricted for a time during the counseling. Sometimes individuals in custody will say, "No one has ever prayed for me like that before." Or they may comment on the prayer, bringing back a recollection from their faith history, or it may cause them to engage in a moment of scriptural/spiritual reflection. When I follow up with individuals a week or two later, they sometimes will mention how they are grateful for the check-up and for the time and conversation and will comment on things that have stuck with them. Also, occasionally CO's (correctional officers) will notice that the interventions have a calming effect and help the person to cope.

What do incarcerated care receivers expect from you as a prison chaplain? Incarcerated individuals hope caregivers have the answers, but realistically chaplains don't. That must be established at the initial contact. However, they expect us to provide a genuine response of faith, forward-looking, and some form of productive opportunity within reach. They expect chaplains to be honest with them and, at the same time, have specific care relegated to them only.

Moving forward, what would you like to see more of from chaplaincy? When collaborating with individuals in custody on their spiritual journey, I operate from a posture of mutuality, where each learns from the other. I don't presume to know or fully understand their journey or that I have all of the answers they need. On the contrary, I assume that I will learn as much from them as they can from me. I have high expectations of those I am collaborating with and seek to hold them accountable for their decisions and the choices they commit to. I choose to empower others as my primary method of care, walking alongside and providing support and encouragement as they take their steps in the journey of healing and transformation.

One of the ideas I came up with while conducting this survey was having a security program that assisted individuals in custody immediately transitioning into a program that suited their needs. While the 3 Cs concept gave space to individuals to express similar concerns each one faced, there wasn't an alternative put in place to assist them in developing that which they most desired. For example, an individual previously expressed the difficulty of participating in classes that would enhance any skill they had.

Furthermore, individuals who are trying to stay away from any drug/alcohol abuse and not having an outlet for prevention result in jeopardizing an opportunity to work towards healing from their trauma. Thus, the design would be collaborating with current volunteers that specialize in the areas of education and drug/alcohol abuse treatment, which enables the individual to have a greater appreciation of what value they must contribute to the discussion of transformation.

Even when it comes to religious programming, they've expressed their contempt for the church or other religious affiliations' inability to put safeguards in place that understand where they came from. They're accustomed to religious organizations shaming them for past actions or any punishment they have gained as a direct result of incarceration. The problem is that religious leaders (particularly the church) have neglected to put in place a space that addresses their spiritual pain. For any religious leader, the concern shouldn't be "what do you use to cope with spiritual pain," but delivering a message of compassion that states, "how can I help you cope with your spiritual pain?" I needed to understand there isn't a special antidote or remedy that one instantly apprehends. Instead, one must journey with individuals with options that help develop them into the spiritually led individual they are.

Along with that, journeying with them becomes essential to their progress. While the recommendation is suitable, they regularly conducted one-on-one checkups once a week or month, providing them the space to express their appreciation for someone within the correctional system, ultimately desiring what's best for them. This even extends to external resources upon release, which in many cases will demonstrate the community is taking the responsibility to nurture and be sensitive enough to accept them for who they are. They are more than individuals with a criminal history; they are human beings striving to find their voice and place in the world. They are more than the perception of what's wrong in society; they are a reflection of our mistreatment toward our neighbors. And they are not the lost generation exempt from redemption but the victims of an unjust system that structurally diminishes their character and potential for rehabilitation.

From a personal endeavor aspect, this becomes a heuristic discovery for them to incorporate into their own lives what is most important. In a lot of cases, they aren't expecting immediate change. Instead, they wanted to focus on pressing toward their transformation and shifting away from previously perceived images of how the public views them. More critical was addressing their spiritual needs. Let me pivot back to the narrative of notice of God and God's existence in their life. It's not the conclusion God doesn't exist but rather a response to the disconnectedness of understanding God's presence during their trauma.

For some, their anger didn't permit them to believe God would appear present during their suffering. For some of them, their trauma restricted them from acknowledging God as being all-powerful or all-knowing. And, for others, God seemed too distant to occupy the same space to their detriment. However, they shifted from that spiritual mindset when grace became the focal point. By this, they've witnessed families heal from the traumatic experience that caused them to be incarcerated, and due to the spiritual transformation taking place within their lives, they conducted an assessment on themselves with "I need to transform for me and become the person God desires me to be."

CONCLUSION

Chaplaincy within the prison setting is not an easy task. Often, there can be moments of discouragement because you're trying to gauge if you feel like you're contributing to someone's transformation. Along with that, working in a system that has individuals in custody usually has discordant opinions as to the type of population we serve. Regardless of their crime, their past behavior or current predicament of wrongful conviction is challenging to navigate. Providing hope to a person that has given up on hope in prison is an exhausting task maneuver. Thus, it becomes a question of the mission one desires for others.

Prison Life and the Aftermath of Thug Living

When I think about my ministry, I struggle with the intentions of others because I've witnessed the vulnerability of individuals in custody. To hear those incarcerated admitting the harm they've caused and not desiring forgiveness is heartbreaking. To listen to those wails within proximity to me, unable to secure their emotional distress and lean on you for support, says there must be something more to life. Their demise is a response to what they are currently processing, and their past still haunts them, making it hard to find any value in what they can cultivate within themselves. There must be room for grace and mercy, even for those incarcerated.

Therefore, let's imagine hearing yourself being sentenced to natural life in prison and being transferred to a facility to reside for the rest of your life, feeling no desire to live. Imagine being placed in a cell with a stranger. You do not know what caused them to become incarcerated. Night falls, and the only thing you can see beyond your six-by-eight-foot cell behind a steel door is a wall you can't reach. Yet you envision that one day, through the foggy window, that a blast of light will give you hope that God hasn't forgotten you. That's what chaplains are and should be, a blast of hope that leads one toward a road of recovery. Be that hope because sometimes they need to see the activity of God in others before they can accept the breath of God in themselves.

Survey for Formerly Incarcerated Individuals

You HAVE BEEN SELECTED to voluntarily partake in a research project in the form of a questionnaire. Your comments will not be shared beyond this project. All information will be used to inform chaplains how to perform pastoral care in a maximum-security, medium-max, and medium prison setting. All participants in this study will not be referred to by name but only a number to identify them. Thus, this study ensures strict confidentiality will be exercised, and all surveys conducted for this research will be destroyed after the date is collected. If you choose to opt out of this survey during this study, your information will be removed and no further information will be used.

The aim of this project is to examine the ways in which pastoral care reaches the hearts and minds of long-term incarcerated men within a maximum-security, medium-max, and medium prison setting during their times of despair. Pastoral care is going to be given close examination as to how chaplains properly deliver messages of care to those currently incarcerated. Therefore, the project is focused on preparing chaplains for the next-level care and tools they needed to be effective in providing spiritual care. This case study will consist of five to ten chaplains, who provide care to those sentenced from twenty years to natural life. This study will show the effectiveness (or

lack thereof) of how pastoral care has significance to those incarcerated and how it can revitalize their spiritual identity to
become whole. Furthermore, this study will raise awareness for
chaplains as to how various theological concepts influence the
atmosphere of those serving long-term sentences. All resulting
applicable methods will help train future chaplains to carry out
missions of care.

Please answer the following questions listed below and return to
the Chaplain Damien Davis at damiendavis11@gmail.com. If you
choose not to participate, please contact Chaplain Davis, so he can
remove your survey from the research project.

How effective was the pastoral care you received while
incarcerated?

In what specific ways was it helpful and/or in what specific ways
was it not helpful?

What evidence do you have that your pastoral care needs were
met?

What methods have you found helpful to obtain the care you
needed, and what feedback would you give to chaplains
providing care?

What methods have you found helpful used when you've collaborated with a chaplain on your spiritual journey?

What should chaplains be made aware of when providing care to those incarcerated?

Moving forward, what would you like to see more of from chaplaincy?

Survey for Chaplains

You HAVE BEEN SELECTED to voluntarily partake in a research project in the form of a questionnaire. Your comments will not be shared beyond this project. All information will be used to inform chaplains how to perform pastoral care in a maximum-security, medium-max, and medium prison setting. All participants in this study will not be referred to by name but only a number to identify them. Thus, this study ensures strict confidentiality will be exercised and all surveys conducted for this research will be destroyed after the date is collected. If you choose to opt out of this survey during this study, your information will be removed and no further information will be used.

The aim of this project is to examine the ways in which pastoral care reaches the hearts and minds of long-term incarcerated men within a maximum-security, medium-max, and medium prison setting during their times of despair. Pastoral care is going to be given close examination as to how chaplains properly deliver messages of care to those currently incarcerated. Therefore, the project is focused on preparing chaplains for the next-level care and tools they needed to be effective in providing spiritual care. This case study will consist of five to ten chaplains, who provide care to those sentenced from twenty years to natural life. This study will show the effectiveness (or lack thereof) of how pastoral care has significance to those incarcerated and how it can revitalize their spiritual identity to become whole. Furthermore, this study will raise awareness for chaplains as to how various theological concepts influence the atmosphere of those serving long-term sentences. All resulting applicable methods will help train future chaplains to carry out missions of care.

Please answer the following questions listed below and return to the Chaplain Damien Davis at damiendavis11@gmail.com. If you choose not to participate, please contact Chaplain Davis, so he can remove your survey from the research project.

How has the pastoral care you provided been most effective to those incarcerated? Why?

What evidence do you have that your caregiving was effective?

What methods have you used to obtain feedback from those in your care, and what feedback did you receive from the care receivers?

What methods have you used when you've collaborated with an individual in custody's spiritual journey?

What do incarcerated care receivers expect from you as a prison chaplain?

Moving forward, what would you like to see more of from chaplaincy?

Consent Form for Survey

You ARE INVITED TO participate in a web-based online survey regarding how formally incarcerated persons were provided pastoral care, was it helpful and/or hurtful, and how should chaplains provide pastoral care to those currently incarcerated. This is a research project being conducted by Damien Davis, a student at McCormick Theological Seminary. It should take approximately one hour to complete.

PARTICIPATION

Your participation in this survey is voluntary. You may refuse to take part in the research or exit the survey at any time without penalty. You are free to decline to answer any question you do not wish to answer for any reason.

BENEFITS

You will receive no direct benefits from participating in this research study. However, your responses may help us learn more about effective pastoral care to the individuals in custody.

RISKS

For those formerly incarcerated the risk would be reflected in any emotional or spiritual detachment that pastoral care given to you (or lack thereof). This is an individual assessment regarding the effectiveness of pastoral care. To minimize this risk, I will remind you all data collected will be confidential, and your names will not be used beyond this research. You will be provided with therapeutic resources in case you demonstrate the need or request information for more counseling.

CONFIDENTIALITY

Your survey answers will be sent to a link at damiendavis11@ icloud.com where data will be stored in a password-protected electronic format. All data collected, such as your name and email address, will be destroyed after the information is used. Therefore, your responses will remain anonymous. No one will be able to identify you or your answers, and no one will know whether you participated in the study.

At the end of the survey, you will be asked if you are interested in participating in an additional interview by phone or email. If you choose to provide contact information such as your phone number or email address, your survey responses may no longer be anonymous to the researcher. However, no names or identifying information would be included in any publications or presentations based on these data, and your responses to this survey will remain confidential.

CONTACT

If you have questions at any time about the study or the procedures, you may contact my research supervisor, Professor Rev. Dr. Sharon Ellis Davis, via email at sdavis@go.mccormick.edu.

Consent Form for Survey

If you feel you have not been treated according to the descriptions in this form, or that your rights as a participant in research have not been honored during the course of this project, or you have any questions, concerns, or complaints that you wish to address to someone other than the investigator, you may contact the Rev. Dr. Stephanie Crumpton, Associate Professor of Practical Theology at scrumpton@mccormick.edu.

ELECTRONIC CONSENT

Please select your choice below. You may print a copy of this consent form for your records. Clicking on the "Agree" button indicates that

- You have read the above information
- You voluntarily agree to participate
- You are 18 years of age or older

(Agree)

(Disagree)

Consent Form for Survey

The following information is a gathering of data based on survey questions directed toward formally incarcerated persons provided me with evidence-based research on how pastoral care has been helpful and/or hurtful to them.

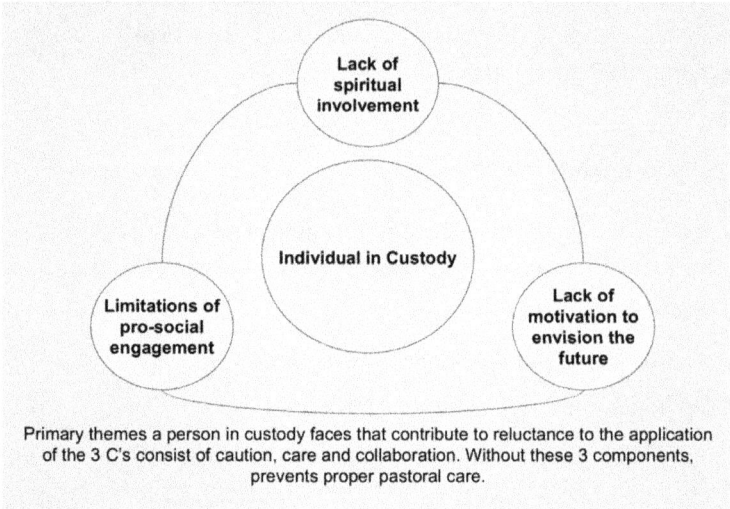

Primary themes a person in custody faces that contribute to reluctance to the application of the 3 C's consist of caution, care and collaboration. Without these 3 components, prevents proper pastoral care.

The 3 Cs concept: Caution, Care and Collaboration

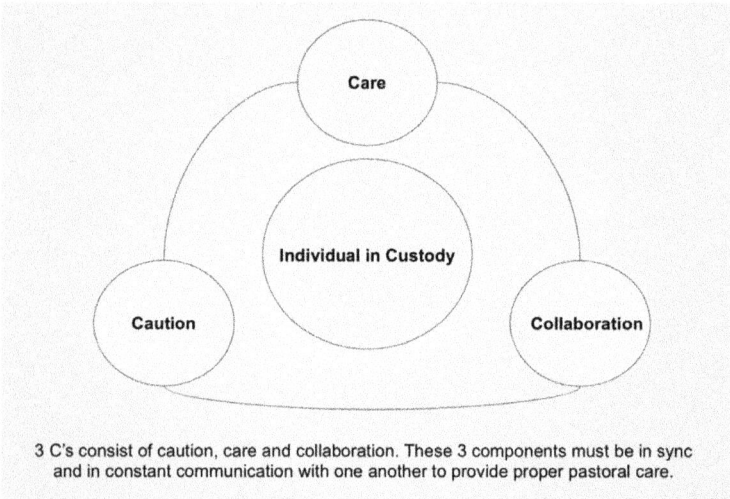

3 C's consist of caution, care and collaboration. These 3 components must be in sync and in constant communication with one another to provide proper pastoral care.

Bibliography

Anderson, Ray S. *The Shape of Practical Theology: Empowering Ministry with Theological Praxis*. Downers Grove, IL: InterVarsity, 2001.

Badke, William. *Research Strategies: Finding Your Way through the Information Fog*, 5th ed. Bloomington, IN: iUniverse.com, 2014.

Barkman, Linda Lee Smith. "Towards a Missional Theology of Prison Ministry." Ph.D. diss., Fuller Theological Seminary, 2017.

Brault, Emily R. "Pastoral Care and Counseling in Prison: What Works?" *Journal of Pastoral Care & Counseling* 68.3 (Sep 2014) 1–10. https://doi.org/10.1177/154230501406800306.

Browning, Don S. & Terry D. Cooper. *Religious Thought & The Modern Psychologies*, 2nd ed. Minneapolis: Fortress Press, 2004.

Clifton-Soderstrom, Michelle. "Liberal Arts in Prison: Integrating Live & Liberating Minds," YouTube video, 6:01—6:14. 2017. https://www.youtube.com/watch?v=C6pf1dW9BOk&list=PLI_eQ8rNuOKDKNa0AbqWwV1_AkEW7LDEc

Crenshaw, Kimberlé, "What is Intersectionality?" YouTube video, 1:54, 2017. https://www.youtube.com/watch?v=ViDtnfQ9FHc

Coogan, Michael David, et al. 2010. *The New Oxford Annotated Bible: New Revised Standard Version*. Oxford: Oxford University Press.

Coylar, Julia, and Karris Holley. "Narrative Theory and the Construction of Qualitative Texts," in *New Approaches to Qualitative Research: Wisdom and Uncertainty*, edited by Maggi Savin-Baden and Claire Major. New York: Routledge Taylor & Francis Group, 2010.

Duffy, Maria. *Paul Ricoeur's Pedagogy of Pardon: A Narrative Theory of Memory and Forgetting*. New York: Continuum International Publishing Group, 2009.

Gilliard, Dominique DuBois. *Rethinking Incarceration: Advocating for Justice that Restores*. Downers Grove, IL: InterVarsity, 2017.

Goode, W. Wilson Sr., Charles E. Lewis Jr., Harold Dean Trulear. In *Ministry with Prisoners & Families: The Way Forward*, edited by W. Wilson Goode, Sr. Valley Forge, PA: Judson, 2011.

Bibliography

Hallet, Michael, et al. "U.S. Prison Seminaries: Structural Charity, Religious Establishment, and Neoliberal Corrections." *The Prison Journal* 99.2 (Mar 2019) 150–71. https://doi.org/10.1177/0032885519825490

Holeman, Virginia, and Todd Holeman. *Theology for Better Counseling: Trinitarian Reflections for Healing and Formation.* Downers Grove, IL: InterVarsity, 2012.

Maruna, Shadd, Louise Wilson, and Kathryn Curran. *Why God Is Often Found Behind Bars: Prison Conversions and the Crisis of Self-Narrative.* Research in Human Development 3 (2006) 161–84.

Menakem, Resmaa. *My Grandmother's Hands: Racialized Trauma and the Pathway to Mending Our Hearts and Bodies.* Las Vegas: Central Recovery Press, 2017.

O'Conner, Thomas. "The Impact of a Volunteer Prison Ministry Program on the Long-term Recidivism of Federal Inmates." Mar 16, 2017. https://transformingcorrections.com/the-impact-of-a-volunteer-prison-ministry-program-on-the-long-term-recidivism-of-federal-inmates/

Pounder, Sadie. *Prison Theology: A Theology of Liberation, Hope and Justice.* Dialog. 47. 2008. 10.1111/j.1540–6385.2008.00402. x.

Rambo, Shelly. *Resurrecting Wounds: Living in the Afterlife of Trauma.* Waco. TX: Baylor University Press, 2017.

Sensing, Tim. *Qualitative Research: A Multi-Methods Approach to Projects for Doctor of Ministry Theses.* Eugene, OR: Cascade, 2011.

Simon, Jonathan, and Richard Sparks. *The SAGE Handbook of Punishment and Society.* Los Angeles; London: SAGE, 2013.

Tisdale, Leonora Tubbs. *Prophetic Preaching: A Pastoral Approach.* Louisville: Westminster John Knox Press, 2010.

Trulear, Harold Dean. "Loving the Incarcerated." YouTube video, 17:42, 2015. https://www.youtube.com/watch?v=kWC55w-19r4&t=315s.

Van Der Kolk, Bessel. *The Body Keeps the Score: Brain, Mind, And Body in the Healing of Trauma.* New York: Penguin, 2015.

Index

"absconding," 32
accountability, 19, 27
acts of kindness, 24
advocating for the incarcerated, 28
"afterlife of the cross," 37
"Ahmad" (inmate), 9
alcohol and drug abuse, 5, 52
Anderson, Ray S., 18–19, 18n14,
    19n15
anger, 53
Angola (Louisiana prison), 16
anti-social environments, 38, 41
anxiety, 31
authenticity, 41, 46, 47

Badke, William, 14n4
Barkman, Linda Lee Smith, 16,
    17nn9–10
behaviorism, 21–22
"being present" with/"walking
    alongside" inmates, 13, 37,
    51, 52
"being seen," 13
biases. *See also* stereotypes of
    individuals in custody
    implicit bias, 41
    against individuals in custody,
        3, 4, 23, 25, 29, 31, 32, 48,
        49, 53
    against people of color, 44

"BJ" (inmate)
    analysis of case, 35–42
    author's dialogue with, 34–35
    background, 32–33
    Black communities, 39. *See also*
        people of color
blind forgiveness, 32
Brault, Emily R., 19, 19n18,
    20nn19–20, 21
Browning, Don S., 21, 22n27

care (3 Cs)
    application of, 29, 30, 37
    definition, 24, 39–40
caretakers, chaplains as, 11
caution (3 Cs)
    application of, 29, 30, 36, 37
    definition, 23, 39
cellmates, relationships with, 6, 38
change, 31, 36, 45
chaplaincy
    bringing spirituality to the
        incarcerated, 42, 44, 46
    as caretaking, 11
    Christian influencer role as part
        of, 15, 23
    definition, purpose, and
        expectations, 1, 5, 7, 26, 42
    inmates' views of, 43, 44–47

Index

chaplaincy (*cont.*)
  inmates with no religious
    affiliation and, 45
  one-on-one engagement, 44, 51
  as physical representation of
    God, 46
  psychology and, 10, 15, 23
  surveys of chaplains, 26, 49–54,
    58–60
  3 Cs and, 29
  training for, 47
Christian influencer role in
  chaplaincy, 15, 23
Christian values, 14
Christ-like responses, 37
church affiliations, 29, 42, 43, 45, 48
church leaders, 52
church services, 7, 45, 47
churches, 47, 52
Clifton Soderstrom, Michelle, 19,
  19nn16–17
cognitive-behavioral approach to
  prison ministry, 20
collaboration (3 Cs)
  application of, 29, 30
  chaplains' comments on, 50,
    51, 59
  definition, 24, 40, 41
  inmates feedback on, 45–46, 56
  inmates with no religious
    affiliation and, 45
  hope and, 42
color, people of, 39, 44
community, 6, 47
compassion, showing, 24, 45, 46
conflict resolution, 7
consistency, 25, 45, 47
contextual theology, 18, 26
conversion narratives, 21
Cooper, Terry D., 21, 22n27
correctional officers (CO's), 5, 51
COVID pandemic, 30, 32
Crenshaw, Kimberlé, 12, 12n1
criminal on the cross (New
  Testament), 13, 14

Curran, Kathryn, 16n6

death, 37–38
despair, 6, 7, 13, 37, 42. *See also*
  hopelessness
diets, religious, 7
"dirty pain," 41
disabilities, 46
diversity of incarcerated population,
  29
divine humility, 26
drug and alcohol abuse, 5, 30, 52
Duffy, Maria, 21
duty, compared with empathy, 29

"early release," Jesus Christ's, 39
education, 25, 44, 45, 47, 51
emotions, dealing with, 36, 50
empathy, 2, 27, 29, 31, 35, 43, 44.
  See also identifying with the
  incarcerated
engagement skills, 20
equilibrium, 41
expectations vs. experience, 38–39

faith, 44
faith histories of inmates, 50. *See
  also* religious affiliations
faith-based cognitive-behavioral
  approach to prison ministry,
  20
families of the incarcerated
  care for/healing of, 47, 53
  communication with, 32
  disconnection from, 12, 30, 33,
    36, 37, 41–42, 47
  expectations after release, 38
  financial support from, 5
  guilt for absence from, 38
feedback from inmates, 2, 24, 25, 26,
  29, 43–47, 50, 56
forgiveness, 19, 32, 54
freedom, 5, 8–9, 32
future, how inmates view, 21, 43, 64

Index

Gillard, Dominique DuBois, 17, 17n11
God. *See also* image of God
  belief in/existence of, 53
  as remembering the incarcerated, 7, 26, 54
  trauma and, 26, 37, 39, 43, 53
God-honoring actions, 22, 40
gospel
  giving inmates a glimpse of, 37
  social and political character of, 20
grace, 2, 17, 31, 43, 46, 53, 54
the great reversal, 21
grief, 50
guilt for absence from families, 38

Hallett, Michael, 16, 16n8
Holeman, Todd, 15, 15n5, 22nn28–30, 40, 40nn13–15, 41nn16–17
Holeman, Virginia, 15, 15n5, 22, 22nn28–30, 40, 40nn13–15, 41nn16–17
Holy Spirit, 22, 40
honesty, 51
hope
  fostering, 3, 12, 22, 33, 40, 42, 43, 54
  Jesus Christ and, 14, 19
  value for the incarcerated, 7, 18, 27
hopelessness, 5, 10, 15, 31, 53. *See also* despair
humanistic approach to prison ministry, 14, 43
humanization/acknowledging humanity in others, 6, 26, 27, 31, 32, 52
humility, 26
hygiene, 6

identifying with the incarcerated, 15. *See also* empathy
identity, 10, 16, 20, 21

image of God
  embodying, 41, 46, 48
  seeing inmates as created in, 4, 11, 21, 49, 54
  seeing oneself as created in, 7, 26, 54
implicit bias, 41
initiative-taking, 7
Inmate Ministers (Angola Prison), 16
"insidious trauma," 39
integrity, 46
interfaith approach to prison ministry, 23
interpersonal skills, 20
intersectionality, 12, 13

Jesus Christ, 14, 17, 19, 21, 37, 39, 46
jewelry, religious, 7
Joseph of Egypt (Old Testament), 17

kindness, acts of, 24

"the least of these," the incarcerated as, 48
LGBTQ identity and issues, 8
limitations, recognizing, 24
listening, 2, 24. *See also* stories, inmates'
loneliness/knowing one is not alone, 10
love and compassion, showing, 24, 45, 46

marriage, 7
Maruna, Shadd, 16, 16n6
masculinity, 8
mass incarceration, 13
McBride, Jenny, 20
medical issues among incarcerated, 31
Menakem, Resmaa, 41, 41nn18–20
mental health, 5, 6, 27, 30, 39, 42, 46
mental health professionals, 33
mercy. *See* grace
ministry of presence, 49

Index

monetary assistance, 48
multi-method approach to prison ministry, 13

narrative psychology/theory, 15, 21
narratives, conversion, 21
natural life sentences, 4, 7, 54, 55, 58
normalcy, sense of, 9, 10, 11, 44

O'Conner, Thomas, 16, 16n7
oppressed peoples, the gospel and, 20–21

parole agents, 32
patience, 46
Paul (New Testament), 37
people of color, 39, 44
phones, communication via, 34
physical assault in prisons, 6
positive reinforcement, 21–22
post-traumatic stress disorder (PTSD), 8. *See also* trauma
Pouder, Sadie, 18, 18nn12–13
praxis, 46
prayer, 35, 44, 50
presence, ministry of, 49
prison environment
  chaplains grappling with, 7
  compared with life outside, 8
  effects on mental and spiritual state, 39
  negative anti-social atmosphere, 38, 41
  physical aspects of, 4, 23, 32, 36, 39, 40, 54
prison mentality, not conforming to, 11
privileged peoples, the gospel and, 20–21
pro-social environments, 9, 38, 43, 64. *See also* social networks
psychological damage of incarcerated. *See* trauma
psychology
  chaplaincy and, 10, 15, 23

narrative psychology, 21
  spirituality and, 22, 23, 42
PTSD (post-traumatic stress disorder), 8. *See also* trauma
punishment, 2, 17, 27, 28, 52
purpose, sense of, 6–7

Rambo, Shelly, 37–38, 38nn5–6, 39, 39nn11–12
rape, in prison, 8
rapport with incarcerated, 6. *See also* trust
reactional response/reactive coping, 7, 37, 41
recidivism, 13, 33, 47
redemption, inmates as worthy of, 17. *See also* self-worth
reflection of society's failures, the incarcerated as, 52
rehabilitation/reformation, 13, 14, 16, 18, 53
release from incarceration and re-entry into society, 5, 6, 9, 25, 37, 47, 52
religious affiliations, 29, 42, 43, 45, 48, 50
religious diets, 7
religious diversity, 29
religious jewelry, 7
religious leaders, 52
religious organizations, 47, 52
religious services, 7, 45, 47
resources for the incarcerated, 44, 45, 47, 50
respect, 10, 47
"restricted housing," 28

sacredness, sense of, 42, 50
scriptures, 51
security program, 51–52
self-accountability, 19, 27
self-assessment/self-reflection, 19–20, 39
self-care/self-love, 11, 41

Index

self-identity/self-narrative, 10, 16,
  20, 21
self-worth, 6, 9, 17, 30, 39
Sensing, Tim, 13n3, 15
shame, from religious organizations,
  52
sin, blaming individuals' conditions
  on, 22
Skinner, B. F., 21–22
social and political character of the
  gospel, 20
social networks, 19. *See also* pro-
  social environments
Soli Deo Gloria (glory to God
  alone), 26
spiritual care, 42, 44, 48, 58
spiritual health, 27, 52
spiritual identity, 56, 59
spiritual journey theme, 46, 50, 51,
  56, 59
stereotypes of individuals in
  custody, 4, 8, 25, 29, 53. *See
  also* biases
stories, inmates', 2, 24, 27, 50. *see
  also* conversion narratives;
  narrative psychology/theory
suicide, 9
Sunday services, 7, 45
surveys
  of chaplains, 26, 49–54, 58–60
  consent form, 61–63
  design of, 25
  of formerly incarcerated, 25–26,
    44–48, 55–57
  sample questions, 44–47, 49–51,
    56–57, 59–60

theology, 11, 18, 22, 26
therapeutic agenda, incarceration
  as, 15
3 Cs
  application of, 28, 29, 33, 36, 41
  definition and introduction to,
    2, 3, 10, 23–25, 42
  diagram, 64

in surveys, 25, 49, 51
"thug life," 1
Tisdale, Leonora Tubbs, 37n4
trans-cultural approach to prison
  ministry, 11
transition to leaving prison, 9, 25,
  37, 47, 52
trauma
  addressing/acknowledging, 6,
    27, 31, 50
  being accustomed to, 9
  caring for those with, 31, 32, 33,
    36, 40, 41
  coping with, 20, 41
  God and, 26, 43, 53
  healing from, 52, 53
  identity and, 27
  during incarceration, 46, 48
  "insidious trauma," 39
  negative impacts of, 8, 27, 30, 41
  prior to incarceration, 10, 48
  resisting re-traumatizing, 33
trauma gap, 38–39
Trulear, Harold Dean, 20, 20nn21–
  22, 38–39, 38nn7–9, 39n10
trust, 2, 6, 14, 21, 45, 47, 49

value, inmates' sense of, 6, 9, 17,
  30, 39
Van Der Kolk, Bessel, 36, 36nn1–2
victims, the incarcerated as, 53
violence, 7, 30

"walking alongside"/"being present"
  with inmates, 13, 37, 51, 52
When They See Us (film), 46
whole, working towards being, 27
Wilson, Louise, 16n6
worth, inmates recognizing their
  own, 6, 9, 17, 30, 39
wounds, depicted as human
  weakness, 39
wrongful convictions, 17, 53

Zoom meetings, 32, 34

71